Still Climbing

Still Climbing

Betty Roberts

ISBN: 978-1-956074-54-3 (Paperback Edition)
ISBN: 978-1-956074-55-0 (Hardcover Edition)
ISBN: 978-1-956074-53-6 (E-book Edition)

Book Ordering Information

Phone Number: 315 288-7939 ext. 1000 or 347-901-4920
Email: info@globalsummithouse.com
Global Summit House
www.globalsummithouse.com

Printed in the United States of America

Title of Other Works by Betty Roberts

- ❖ In the Shadow of the Bridge
- ❖ Midnight Chronicles: A Love Story
- ❖ Leaning into the Wind: The Wilderness of Widowhood (writing as Betty Bryant)
- ❖ Short story "Cave In" Published in the Scribbler, University of Alabama in Huntsville, Alabama (writing as Betty Osborne)

In Memory of
my parents
Wallace Bryant Phipps
(7/13/99-1/16/88)
and
Grace Etta Jackson Phipps
(4/2/05-8/3/76)

DEDICATION

Thou reader throbbest
life and pride and love the same as I,
Therefore, for thee the following chants.
~Walt Whitman (1819-1892)
in "Leaves of Grass"

ACKNOWLEDGEMENT

Still Climbing is a combination of fiction and fact, a biographical story interrupted by short stories which are fiction. When asked if the book is fiction or fact, the only answer is "both".

ONE

Materials

For as the material of the Carpenter
Is wood,

And of a Sculptor,
Stone,

So is the material for living
Each man's own.

~Betty Roberts

Betty Lou Phipps
Junior High School

Betty Lou Phipps

High School Graduation
Matoaka High School
Matoaka, West Virginia

Betty Lou Phipps
University of Virginia
School of Nursing Graduation
Charlottesville, Virginia

According to legend, when I was two years old, I pulled the drawers out of the kitchen cabinet, used them as a ladder, and climbed up to sit on the top of the cabinet, only a few inches from the ceiling. About the age of four, I climbed out the bedroom window of our two-story house, sat on the roof of the back porch, and called down to my mother who was hanging clothes on the backyard clothesline, "Hey, Ma-Ma, Look at me!"

Mother calmly answered, "Go back in the window, Betty Lou, and come down here. I'll give you a cookie!" I did as I was told and got my cookie. Due to a somewhat vague diagnosis of "Saint Vitus's Dance" shortly after birth, Mother was afraid to spank me, afraid it would trigger the extreme agitation and nervous twitching I had exhibited after birth and for the first year of my life.

By the time I was five, I would run to the passenger station, a distance of a mile or so, to see the Station operator who kept lime green suckers in a blue Mason jar. This required walking along the railroad tracks, usually on the shiny rail itself, and Mother lived in fear of my getting hit by a train. She started house-hunting away from the railroad, and nearly a year later we moved to a small town "up the road", where the railroad crossed over the town, and where Betty surely would not venture on the tracks.

According to historical (hysterical) research, the first Short Stories were written by a man called AESOP, a slave, who must have also been a farmer, a zoo-keeper, and owned a Pet Shop on the side, since all of his stories were told by talking animals or birds. One of his short stories goes something like this:

THE CROW AND THE PITCHER

Once upon a time there was a great big black bird and some people called him a "Crow" although he was never known to crow—that was done by his friend, the Rooster. The Crow had been traveling a long distance and couldn't get off I-95 to get a drink of water. After many hours, he spotted a large vessel by the side of the road. At first, he thought it was a McDonalds, but then realized there was no golden arch. Too late to get back in traffic, he took the exit off, and returned to the large vessel. He put on the brakes and coasted to a stop, dragging his tail feathers in the dirt.

The vessel was as large as he, but by raising on his claw-tips he could peer into the top. Yes! By George! There was water in the jug. He tried to put his beak down into the water but could not reach it.

He stepped back, put his beak under his wing, crossed his legs and leaned against the jug. If he could hover—but no, that was patented by that little bitty fellow, what was his name? Oh, yes, the Hummingbird. Everyone said he couldn't carry a tune in a bucket –a bucket! That's what he needed. He could tip the jug over and pour the water in the bucket; his beak would go into the bucket. He looked about. No buckets, just rocks. Yes! He could stack the rocks to stand on, but no. These were all little rocks.

Suddenly a light bulb came on over his head. He had an idea! He picked up a small rock, dropped it, peered into the jug, yes, the water had come up a little. He dropped another, that's better, another rock, another, anotheranotheranother –there was the water! It was cool and he drank and drank and finally, saved by the Bell –but no – saved by the pebbles, he sat up and looked around. The traffic on I-95 was bumper-to-bumper, too crowded to get back on, but he had heard of another north-south route, just a few miles West, as the crow flies. If he remembered correctly, it was called I-75. He could try that. No longer thirsty, he took to the air, dragging his tail feathers in the dust again, and turned right.

Moral of the story: Necessity is the mother of invention.

This will be my third book in as many years (third pebble?). I make no apologies for my writing; it is my "busy work" and I have yet to reach the water. I write because I must, have always "had to", the natural outreach of a voracious reader. Success has little to do with it, ambition, yes, but success, no. As every writer knows, success is just around the corner, with the next book, the next story: the next pebble dropped in the water might make economic waves.

There was another writer (storyteller) who figured prominently in my early years. I never learned his first name, but he was kin. He was my Uncle. Uncle Remus. He liked to tell stories about animals too, but I think AESOP had a bigger barnyard. I was in about the second grade when I wrote the following poem which featured Uncle Remus characters:

BRER FOX, BRER RABBIT AND THE TAR BABY

Old Brer Fox said, "It's such a pretty day,
I'm sure Brer Rabbit will be a'comin' this way.
That's one rabbit I'se determined to git,
And I ain't caught him yet!"

"Brer Bear," says Old Brer Fox,
"I've got sense, yes, lots,
"I'll fool that ole rabbit yet,
I'll make a Tar Baby—it's the best plan
I could get."

He made the Tar Baby,
And sat it on the path.
Then hid himself and
Got ready to laugh.

Down the road came the Bunny,
As happy as a bear in a pot of honey.
"Hi there," said Brer Rabbit, "a fine day!"
The Tar Baby said nothing—
He shouldn't act that way!

Brer Rabbit turned around. "Hi, he said,
The Tar baby didn't make a sound.
"I'll slap you!" The Rabbit said
And he slapped him on the head.

"Let me loose, you Tar Baby!
Why can't you act like a lady?"
The rabbit danced all around
But only one foot was on the ground.

Out came Brer Fox, holding his side,
"I've got you now," He cried.
But the sun came out and melted the tar,
Brer Rabbit was loose, like a shooting star!

We had moved up the road a few miles and the new house had a wide front porch with a railing that went all the way around, perfect for walking. When Mother ordered me off of it for the third time, I got my first switching, after which I was careful not to be caught. Mother had her own home-grown switching tree, a giant willow that straddled the fence with my teacher's yard. My teacher was a great book-reader, and he unselfishly loaned all his new books to us just as soon as he had read them; thus my reading library was replenished frequently and with books far over my head. Later, my sister, four-years older than I, checked books out at her high school library and before she returned them, I read those also.

The following quote from Mr. Thomas Jefferson breaks my heart: "The most valuable of talents is that of never using two words when one will do."

The truth is, I dearly love adjectives, words like, "beautiful, gorgeous, attractive, pretty, captivating" –I could go on, but you get the idea, the heart, the theme. Eons –ages, years, an eternity—ago, when I was a child—a tyke, a kid, lass, brat, juvenile, rug-rat—I was told that I was ugly—homely, an eyesore, revolting – by my sister – relative, sibling, family – all right, Mr. Jefferson, you win. What I said, in the preceding paragraph was, "When I was a child, my sister called me ugly."

At this time, I was writing romantic stories about ugly girls who met their prince and suddenly became lovely. Fortunately, these stories, which I kept hidden under my mattress, didn't survive. And, at this age, my mother decided I would become a nurse. She made this call because I was forever putting bandages on my dolls and taking them to the doctor, perhaps playing as a reflection of my own life. Every winter I had tonsillitis or pneumonia, as did my younger sister. The long hours in bed contributed to our preoccupation with books –any book, every book.

By the age of ten, I had learned that all Airline Stewardesses were required to be R.N.'s. My not-so-secret ambition was to fly, and the only way I could do that was to become an R.N. and a stewardess. My title would be Miss Betty Phipps, R.N.

My older sister had beautiful black hair, like both of our parents, while mine was skimpy, dish-water brown and unbelievably straight. So impossible to keep looking good, Mother kept it cut short, and I was skinny beyond belief, burning my daily calories in excessive energy. My sister, June, sang like a bird (a lark? no, more like a Mockingbird with great versatility) before I could talk, and while I was learning to carry a tune, she was learning to play the piano. It was not until I turned twelve that we realized I was a born alto and was learning to harmonize. By that time, my sister had convinced me I was, indeed, ugly. If it had not been for Uncle Dan, there's no telling how old I would have been before that opinion of myself was corrected. Uncle Dan had married my mother's youngest sister, who was only three years older than my sister, then sixteen. I was the brat (one word will do) who wanted to follow them about, be included with the grown-ups. My sister had been a grown up from the age of four, but at twelve, I was still just a 'brat'.

Uncle Dan had been drafted. He owned a one-man gasoline distribution business and going into the Army would close it —unless Aunt Bea could keep it open. Mother and Dad allowed big sister to spend the summer away from home, keeping the office open while Aunt Bea drove the delivery truck. Before shipping out, Uncle Dan and Aunt Bea came to visit us. He was handsome in his uniform and a great "cut-up", a fun young man and I was captivated. After dinner we gathered around the piano and sang all the Hit Parade favorites.

Mother went to the kitchen, calling me to come help her prepare desert. At one point she asked me to get something from the pantry —the pantry was a large storage area built under the stairs to the second floor, with the door opening into the kitchen. Uncle Dan came into the kitchen, and like it was yesterday, I recall his words to mother. "Grace," he said, "You are going to have to watch that Betty Lou. When she grows up

9

you will have to fight the boys off with a stick! She's going to be a real charmer!"

Mother had answered briefly, "You think so?" and had changed the subject. I remember standing still, in the pantry, as Dan asked her if she needed any help, and her short negative reply. By the time I came out of the pantry Dan had returned to the singing in the living room. Dan fought in France and returned home. He built his business to be quite successful, branched into real estate, and became the Mayor of his city. Every year he returned to France where the French people celebrated their liberator; a statute of him was in the center of the village.

When Dan was past seventy, he heard that my husband and I would be making a trip down to Florida to visit my sister. He arranged to visit at the same time. Over the years we had been close buddies at family reunions with a special connection. His words, spoken when I needed them the most, stayed with me. He never knew what he had done for a skinny, awkward, twelve-year-old, little girl.

Not long after that, I went through teenaged acne with a vengeance and was fighting the coal dust and cinders that filtered down from the high bridge crossing over the houses. Scrubbing my face had been ingrained by then, but that did not help the acne. One Sunday we drove to a neighboring town to have dinner with my Aunt Gladys and Uncle Audnia. They had no children and Aunt Gladys came to stay with Mother each time she had a baby. Uncle Audnia was a railroader, but, unlike my father, he wore a white dress shirt and tie, and spent all day before a giant board, giving orders for train movement. He was a Dispatcher.

My Dad wore sixteen-inch laced up boots with his britches tucked in and work shirts. He spent his days climbing the electrical poles, either putting up or taking down the high-voltage wiring that ran the electrical engines on the Virginian railroad.

Gladys and Audnia lived in a second-floor apartment overlooking the river. There was a tiny balcony off the kitchen, but it had no staircase, just a little porch where Aunt Gladys hung her mop on the railing to dry. The kitchen was very tiny, and with Mother, June, and Gladys cooking dinner, there wasn't room for me and I was told to "get out of the way." I stepped out on the tiny balcony where I could look right down into the river. There was little water and great gray rocks covered the riverbed; birds perched on the rocks in the sun. Overhead buzzards floated with the upper air currents, moving lazily and free. I was deep into daydreaming about flying with them when Mother realized where I was. "Betty Lou! Get in here! If you fell from there, you'd be killed!"

In my mind, there was no reason I would fall, I wasn't walking the railing, just standing there with a gentle breeze and a wonderful view of the world. There was never room to argue with Mother; I came in. In the living room there was a couch, an easy chair and a coffee table and just walking space between them. Uncle Audnia and Daddy were sitting on the couch, talking railroad, and my younger sister was curled up in the easy chair sound asleep. I sat down beside Daddy and he put his arm around me, his fingers finding my forehead, in what started as a caress, until he felt the bumps and blemishes on my skin. Without missing a beat in what he was saying, he turned my face toward him. "Good Grief! What's wrong with your face? You need to go wash it right now!"

I gladly escaped to the tiny bathroom, and it, like the rest of the apartment, was beautifully decorated, pink towels, sweet-smelling soap, flowers in a pink vase, and three bright lights over a gold-trimmed mirror. By sitting on the tiny sink, I could get my face close to the mirror, under the brightest lights

I'd ever seen. I proceeded to remove digitally every bump and blackhead, leaving a red-splotched face in the height of raging hormonal teenaged acne.

When dinner was called, I wanted to stay in the bathroom, but of course, I couldn't. My parents were horrified when they saw what I had done. June and Red burst out laughing. Aunt Gladys was speechless, sitting with her mouth open. Uncle Audnia put his arm around my shoulders and drew me out of the room with him, saying, "I think I have something that might help." We went back to the tiny bathroom and he opened the cabinet behind the gold mirror and brought out a green glass bottle. "I use this all the time," he said. "Now it will sting at first, but then it will feel real cool. I had the same thing when I was a teenager. It won't last long." After that, it wasn't just Uncle Audnia, it was MY Uncle Audnia.

A few months passed and Aunt Gladys had to have surgery. They had moved to Bluefield, Uncle Audnia moving up in the management of the railroad, and they had bought a two-story house. Aunt Gladys couldn't go up and down stairs, so arrangements were made for me to stay with her to help with meals and housework. She taught me how to iron white dress shirts to look like they had just come from a Chinese laundry, a skill I used the rest of my life, and on Saturday Uncle Audnia took me to see the professional baseball game, complete with hot dogs, popcorn, and all the trimmings. That was my first baseball game, and I never again enjoyed one as much as I did that one. At night I had access to a whole bookcase full of books I hadn't already read, something that had never happened before.

We grew up with Aunt Gladys and Uncle Audnia present for most holidays and frequent Sunday dinners. They never had children of their own; we were their family. Years later, after I graduated nurses training, my first job was as scrub nurse to the neurosurgeon at Bluefield Hospital. Uncle Audnia had a model railroad built in the basement of his house, an elaborate circular table with stations and signals and real lights on the locomotives, a grown-up's toy, one we were not allowed to touch. He was a tall man, over six-foot, and when he would go down to the basement he would sometimes forget to duck, striking his forehead on the crosspiece. He developed a brain tumor that gradually increased to the size of a goose egg on the front of his forehead. One day, after I had been working in O.R. for some time, he sent word for me to come to see him. My new husband and I went one evening, and Aunt Gladys cooked dinner for us. Uncle Audnia wore a baseball cap all through dinner, but finally, after we had eaten and were talked out, he removed his cap. I was shocked at how the bump had grown. Almost child-like, he asked what I thought he should do. Without hesitation, I told him, you come to my boss's office in the morning, and then do whatever he recommends. "Will you be there?" he asked. "Yes, I'll meet you there, and I'll be there when we get this taken care of."

The neurosurgeon cut a bone flap out of the top of his skull, removed the tumor, and sewed the skin flap back over the brain. He no longer had any protection for the brain, so he wore his ball cap all the time. When we brought our rowdy brood home he would find a corner to sit in, away from any chance of injury, and wear his cap. He was fortunate; there was no damage to his nervous system, no brain impairment, and he died years later from an unrelated illness.

Over the years, I've thought about my first experience with a shaving astringent, but we never discussed it again. When my teenagers came along, I often used it for them, but somehow most of them sailed through those years without serious problems.

There was another relative who had a strong influence on my reading, and subsequence writing. Aunt Margie was my Dad's sister. An old maid schoolteacher, she had taken care of both of her parents—my grandparents—until their deaths and had inherited the family farm and home. We made frequent trips to see her, and to gather produce to take back to West Virginia. One summer, when I was ten years old, my parents took me to Virginia to stay with Aunt Margie, to help her with the garden and canning. Green beans and tomatoes were a staple for our winter meals, and I would take home whatever I gathered and canned for my family to use. It was the first time I had been away from my Mom and Dad, and I felt very grown up when they pulled out in the 1938 gray Ford and left me waving good-by. I was to stay a whole week because Daddy couldn't come to get me until his next days off.

During this week, the polio epidemic hit the nation with a vengeance, and I was quarantined. State Troopers stood guard on the highways at state lines. We were not permitted to go in or out of state. All movies and churches were closed, stores permitted only one person at a time to enter. I had cousins who lived next door, and I could play with them, but the problem was, I didn't want to play with them!

The girl, who was my age, was bossy, and no fun after a few minutes, and the boy was younger, much too young to be a playmate. After all, I was practically a grown-up, staying away from home a whole week without my mother. The week turned into three weeks before the curfew was lifted, and Mom and Dad came back to get me. Home never looked so good as it did the day I got back. I remember the shine on the hall table, the dim lighting in the living room with the shades drawn against the summer heat, the sparkle of the windows—the house was spotless in honor of my "home-coming".

I remember, too, the compliments I got as they unloaded nearly one hundred cans of vegetables and fruits, all canned by Betty, with Aunt Margie's guidance. But the best part of the polio quarantine was, Aunt Margie had a basement library, shelves built all around the wall, full of books. As a schoolteacher, she bought books constantly and I spent hours in an old armchair in her basement, reading. She had all of Zane Gray's books, and many other authors, getting all the new releases. With only herself to read them, they were just like new, even smelled new. She allowed me to borrow my favorites to take home with me. Aunt Margie lived to be ninety-eight, lost her sight, but she still enjoyed audio books right to the end.

We moved from the coal camp to a farm the spring June graduated from high school; it was my first year in high school. Clean air, space to breathe, but I missed seeing the high steel bridge. I didn't miss the cinders that fell from the coal cars into my hair.

It was my good fortune to have an excellent English teacher when I entered the new high school. She was a Harvard grad, loved Shakespeare, and had the teaching ability to transfer that love to me, and others. When I went to tenth grade, she asked for me to be her student assistant, which I was allowed to do instead of staying in Study Hall. I helped with passing out assignments, grading papers, and sometimes read passages to the ninth graders while my teacher sat at her desk, chin in her hands, and listened. She was quick to correct me as needed, and after the first few times the ninth graders stopped snickering and listened too. In the eleventh grade we studied literature, and I had found my first love.

Meanwhile, back at the farm, my mother continued with her efforts to get me into Nursing, and our Vet happened to be a University of Virginia graduate. She learned I would need sponsorship by a UVA grad in order to apply, and the Vet

Doctor was quick to volunteer. After all, when he came to look after our cows and calves, I was right there to assist him; he took it for granted I wanted to be a nurse. Many times, I tried to tell my parents I had decided I wanted to change to teaching, and to be a writer. They passed over my comments, went on saving money and selling the calves I was helping to raise. Mother's stock reply, whenever I brought up the subject, was, "You can't make a living being a writer." End of discussion.

During my senior year I was appointed by the principal to be co-editor of the school paper. The boy appointed as my "co-editor" played basketball and helped me with the sports write-ups. He was from the "town" in-crowd, and the other "townies" had to accept me, but they all let me know I got the position because I had been the English teacher's "pet" for the past three years. I loved the job, set up the paper, and generally ran it to suit myself, assigning articles to be written by others on the staff, but always writing the editorial myself. At graduation, I was presented with the Medal for Journalism Senior Award.

My mother was proud of me, a nice "school activity" since I couldn't play basketball. I couldn't attend practice or the games because I lived out of town and Daddy had to have the car in case the railroad had an emergency. Plans for Nursing school continued, and I told myself, it's a way to get to fly. I had no inkling how very difficult it would be, or how badly I would want out of it, until I'd been there several months. And my mother was so proud....

The farm lay in a small valley, bordered on one side by the Bluestone river, by a country road on two sides, leaving only one side to share a common fence line with our neighbors. An extra, wooded hillside lay on the other side of the road, so steep it was only good for harvesting hardwood when they needed it. About the time Dad retired, they cut some of that mature hardwood and built a church down by the highway, a badly needed facility and a donation from my parents to their community. While I was on the farm, it was the best place to go squirrel hunting, thick undergrowth, many old oaks with a generous crop of acorns.

The first summer we were there, we were the main attraction for the neighbors: who ever heard of a farm being worked by women? It was well known that Daddy was a railroad man who was gone more than he was home. Yet, here were these girls, out there cutting hay and shocking it, and Oats! We had a bountiful crop, but it takes a real farmer to stack oats, so it won't take water and rot. Some of the men, being good neighbors, offered to stack the oats and they got their noses out of joint when Mother refused. She wouldn't accept their help without paying for their labor, and our budget was too limited to pay them. Solution: Do it ourselves. And do it, we did. Mother went up to Princeton, to the U.S. Farm Bureau and got a pamphlet put out by the government; we followed directions and our stack of oats turned water just fine, furnishing cattle feed all winter.

Not long after we moved to the farm, Dad took a bad fall on the railroad and injured his back. The doctor was almost positive he had fractured a disc. They took a closet door down, used it as a back-board, and put him to bed for six weeks. Just before his fall, he had plowed an eight-acre field and planted corn. Now, with him out of commission, it was left up to me to take care of the corn field. We had a small garden tractor, gasoline-powered, but I had to walk behind it and guide it by hand. Every morning I got up early, before it got hot, and plowed between the rows, then walked the rows and hand-pulled the weeds between the stalks of corn, pulling off the suckers at the same time. It took a lot of walking to plow and weed eight acres, but we had a bumper crop of corn, and the foliage was stacked for cattle feed through the winter. The corn patch was my baby, for June was in secretarial school, leaving each morning with a neighbor to get to Princeton, then riding the bus to Bluefield college.

My sister, Wilma, was two years younger than I and already a better cook which eventually became her main chore. She was nicknamed "Red" due to her bright red hair. She was also extremely allergic to everything-bees, poison oak, weeds- so she stayed in the house and did the cooking, the dishes, and helped Mother with the canning. Mother and I took care of the cattle and everything outside. Mother also spent much of her day being nursemaid to Daddy.

The neighbors would drive around the road, sometimes stopping to watch what we were doing, shake their heads and predict disaster. We would sing when we were in the fields, especially while shucking corn or bailing hay, and they would stop on the road, and listen. We were "City Folks", and we would fall on our faces before winter. We disappointed them as our farm grew and prospered, the cattle multiplied, the fifty-year old farmhouse was remodeled and painted, dilapidated shacks were removed, and, later, the house was bricked.

Mother's magic touch extended to a large garden with fruit trees, berry bushes, and all the vegetables she knew. They flourished in the old, well-manured soil, and across the front of the vegetable garden she planted all the flowers she had dreamed about planting in the coal camp.

Dad recovered, and returned to the railroad, coming home at night, and picking up farm chores we had been unable to do.

Having always been a church-going family, except for Daddy, we found the closest church to the farm immediately. It happened to be Presbyterian rather than Methodist, but that didn't matter. It didn't take long for folks to find out how well June played the piano and soon she was playing for services,

Mom was directing the choir, and we were there every Sunday morning without fail. As usual, Church was followed by a big Sunday dinner.

One of the first things we learned from our neighbors was about the skating rink, and every Saturday night the young people went roller skating. Never having skated in our small coal camp, we were thrilled to be invited to go with them.

The skating rink was combined with a bowling alley extending down the length of the building. Some of the boys, showing off, would skate for a while, then, without removing their skates, would go around to the bowling alley and bowl with skates on. The girls would gather at the wire fence that separated the two areas and watch.

On our first visit, June had several of the boys offering to help her learn to skate, and it wasn't long before a tall, dark-haired boy—no, make that a man—took over the task. When the rink closed, we went home with our neighbors, the way we had come.

The next morning, a bright Sunday morning in June, we went to church as usual. Just before the service started, here came two of the young men from the skating rink. June asked Mother if they could come home with us for Sunday dinner, and thus began the courtship of my sister and future brother-in-law and a marriage that lasted over fifty years.

I was too young to "date," not yet fifteen, but Mother wouldn't let June go out alone with a boy, so I had to go as "chaperone", and, of course, the "friend" of my to-be brother-in-law had to go too. The four of us went to the skating rink, to the movies, to evening services, and singings all over the area.

By the end of the summer, I was "in love" but not with a high school boy. My heartthrob had graduated high school, was working as an electrician in the coal mines with his father. He had money to spend, his own car, he smoked. He wasn't a "boy", he was a man and four years older than I.

I remember one morning, very early in the morning –corn shucks easier while it is wet with dew—we were sitting in the middle of my corn field, Mother, Red, and I, shucking corn, and I asked Mother how old I had to be to get married. She laughed and asked if I was thinking about getting married, and I answered her, dead-serious.

"Yes, I'm thinking about it," I said. "I just want to know how many years I have to wait."

"Well," Mother said, "Three years of high school, three years of nurses training, a couple of years to find the right man..."

"Eight years? Why I'll be an old maid by then!"

Mother laughed again. She was a large woman, and when she laughed, she laughed all over. "You can't get married until you have an education and can make a living for you and your children," she said.

"My husband will make the living," I said, with the picture of my present 'young man' clearly in my head.

"You never know," my mother said. "What I hope for each of my daughters is that they will be independent, so if they have to earn their own living, they can do so. June is well on her way to doing that. You two must plan your lives like that, too. You never know what will happen."

It was prophetic, those plans expressed by my mother, all those years ago. I and my three sisters, all have had to make the living for ourselves and for our children, at one time or another. I haven't forgotten her words.

Before June settled into a "going steady" situation with the boy from the skating rink, she had other opportunities to date. Shortly after we moved to the farm, Mother joined three other adults and formed a quartet. They sang at singing get-togethers and at other churches, usually for evening services. June, as their accompanist, always went along, and the three younger girls could not be left at home alone. Daddy could be called out to work at any moment if "some fool engineer jumped his train off the track" (Daddy's standard words).

One of the quartet members had a son who had recently enlisted in the Army. This boy came home on leave and the first thing he did was ask June out. True to Mother's regulations, June could go, if Betty went along as chaperone. Nothing was said about him having a 'buddy' come home with him. Still, when the visiting soldier was introduced, my mother, believing so strongly in "safety in numbers", didn't question it when she was told we were going to "the movies." Nothing was said about it being a Drive-In Movie. There hadn't been such a "den of inequity" in the remote Wyoming county and June and I had not been to the one in Mercer county. Since June's date was doing the driving, that put me in the back seat with an enlisted man, out on his first furlong is several weeks.

He wasn't bad looking, just a little 'different', some Italian in his small build and slender face. I thought he was a local boy until he started talking, but when he did, his accent was so strong I could hardly understand him. I quickly learned he was from Brooklyn, New York. To me, New York meant New York City, tall buildings, crowded streets, subways and busses and eating at railroad-car diners. He did most of the talking, in a rapid run of words; it took some time for me to understand him. He was telling me his favorite activity was horse-back riding, and he couldn't understand how I could live on a farm without horses! Frankly, I didn't understand either, except that when we had asked for a pony, mother had said No, and when Mother said no, that meant, no. And Brooklyn? Brooklyn was a Bridge, a big bridge that everyone was always wanting to sell.

While June fought off her date in the front seat, this stranger from a foreign land and I sat congenially in the back seat and talked. Truthfully, I can't recall what movie we saw, but afterward we went to a drive-in restaurant and had cokes and chips while the boys ate full meals. By the time we left the drive-in, and drove the ten miles home, I was dying to go to the bathroom.

We pulled up in front of the house, and when I started to get out of the car, having already thanked my 'date' with a polite handshake, June said, "Don't go in yet!" and her date, sitting in the front seat, promptly locked all the doors! Needing to pee so badly, I started to get out, and couldn't. The boys were begging me to stay, because if I went in, June would have to go in too.

Too naïve, too embarrassed, to tell them why I had to go in, I sat there for a few minutes—until I started peeing in my pants. Then, I hit the boy in the front seat with my purse, reached over his shoulder for the door lock, ran for the front door, straight through the house and out the back door, with urine running down my legs, straight to the "house of many doors."

June had no choice but to come in, and she didn't speak to me for a week, not until she needed a chaperone again.

A quick footnote: The "house of many doors" was our outhouse. When we moved to the farm, one of the first things Dad did was to dig a new pit and demolish the ancient structure used for a toilet. Using six wooden doors he found stored in the barn, he had built a two-holer for us with new wood for the seat because Mother refused to let us sit on the old one: we might "catch" something, and her girls were not going to be put at risk for some unknown disease! There were two doors joined together for the back, two for the front, hinged, so you could open either, and it was one door wide, the end doors nailed tight, quite fancy compared to the one he had torn down.

When Daddy finally hired a plumber to help with installing indoor fixtures, I was in college. It was often referred to as, "Betty's bathroom", due to Mother's argument to Daddy. "What if Betty marries a Doctor. Do you want her to bring a doctor to see us and no bathroom in the house?" At that time, baths were taken in a zinc tub, sitting in the middle of the kitchen floor before the stove, filled with the tea kettle of hot water, just like the residents of our small coal camp had done. But in Wyoming county we'd had an upstairs bathroom with a great big white-enameled, claw-footed tub, and a working commode. We had moved backwards when we traded the 'town house' for the one on the farm!

Graduation, my goal for 12 years, came and went. In the fall I was off to Nurses training in Charlottesville, Virginia, Mr. Thomas Jefferson's college. Mom's dream for me was coming true and my hard curriculum of Latin, Chemistry, and Physics finally ended. Once settled, my journal faithfully recorded daily events about my experiences, notes about the patients, the doctors, and the college "men" we dated, the writing bug alive and well. Those notes are in a box, on a closet shelf, the beginnings of medical novels, patiently waiting until it is their turn to see the light of day.

During my third year of Nursing, I married my first sweetheart who had just returned from Korea. After graduation, we went home to West Virginia, and my name now read, Mrs. Betty Osborne, R.N. My first job was as scrub nurse to the neurosurgeon Uncle Audnia had seen. That 'glorified' position didn't last long, as I became pregnant with our first child and the four-hour scrubs, standing the entire time, made me nauseous and I had to give it up.

There were no day positions available, thus I began 3 to 11 in the emergency room. My new husband would walk several miles down the mountain to meet me when I got off duty. From the hospital we would walk a mile to the bus station, sit at the lunch counter, have cherry pie and ice cream, and catch the midnight bus back up the mountain to our house.

Our baby girl was born a month early, perfect in every way, except her tiny toes lapped over each other and didn't straighten until she began walking. On our way home from the hospital, my mother drove, taking us to the farm where she would help me with the baby and allow me to recover. My husband sat beside her, with me cozily tucked into the back seat with my newborn baby girl. My husband said to my mother, "I'm thinking about going to college. I'm eligible for the G.I. bill and this mining job isn't going to last much longer."

He was "thinking about college"? He had never mentioned it to me! My mother, always enthusiastic about anything educational, responded quickly, "Why, that's a wonderful idea! If you put your application in now, you could start in the fall, Betty will be able to work by then ..." and they worked out all the details while I sat in the back seat and listened. They planned out my life: if I worked evenings, he could take care of little Sunny. He would take day classes, wouldn't have to pay a babysitter. He would go to Montgomery, West Virginia Tech, not as far away as the state University, and he had to stay within the home state ..." He had clearly researched the situation, all without telling me.

We moved to Montgomery during the summer, and he started college in the fall. I had no problem finding a job, my graduation from the University of Virginia assured me that advantage. The only question was, did I want evenings or nights?

Now my new title was, Mrs. Betty Osborne, R.N., Evening Supervisor, and a greener, more inexperienced evening supervisor has rarely been seen. Our schedule for the next five years was arranged around my pregnancies. Work and school,

September through May, then he would find a job for the summer and I would have another baby.

There was a depression in the country during those years and jobs were hard to find, especially in the coal fields. One summer my husband and a buddy left West Virginia, traveling north, stopping in every large city to look for work. It was not until they reached Toledo, on the banks of Lake Erie, that they found work. Answering an ad in the newspaper, the two young men, both ex-G.I.'s, applied for a job on the New York Central railroad and were hired. My husband often told the story of his first day at work. He had been hired as an electrician on the train engines. The first day on the job he was to work with an older, experienced electrician. It was obvious to the older man that my husband had never been on a train engine, and the older man questioned him.

"You've never been on a train, have you?" "No, Sir." My husband said. "And you don't know a damn thing about train engines." "No, Sir," my husband replied, "But I can learn." He got the job, and instead of just the summer months, we spent a year in Ohio, returning to school the next summer.

Even with limited time and training, some of my short stories reflect aspects of our life during those years, stories carefully packed in cardboard boxes each spring, moved for summer jobs, returned to school in the fall, faithfully lugged along with a would-be writer who was rapidly becoming one of the best OB nurses in the area.

Due to the experience gained in the small hospital, I had decided Obstetrics, delivery room specifically, was where I belonged, and we had moved to Beckley. Again, my hours were either evenings or nights; I chose night duty at the Miner's Hospital. The birth rate among the miner's was high and it wasn't long before I passed the one hundred births mark, even though we had a physician on duty during the night.

Five years, and four children later, my husband graduated with a B.S. degree in Education. My resume' more than qualified me for a position in delivery room.

The economic conditions of that time period were reflected in some of my short stories written while employed in Montgomery and Beckley, especially in the one following, titled "Oh My Darlin'".

OH, MY DARLIN'

Ike was a whistlin' man; although he knew the words to the songs, what was in him came out in a low melodious whistle audible only to those nearby. He was mountain-man tall, hard and straight and being a whistling man not much given to talking. Lettie had understood that; Rosemary had not yet caught on. Last night, as they lay in bed, Rosemary had wanted to talk.

"Ike," she'd said, "Ike, let's go all the way to the ocean!"

"Good God, Rosemary! It'd be as damp by the ocean as it is here by the river. Ain't no use goin' if we go all the way to the ocean. "He had pretended to sleep, and she had settled back against his arm. That had been hours ago. Rosemary had gone to sleep curled against him, but he could not sleep, he had thinking to do. Women were all alike. Lettie had wanted to see the ocean too. He'd never give it a thought. There had been no reason to leave, this was home, he figured he had plenty of time, always figured he'd be the first to go, most miners were, either in a rock slide or black lung, and the women lived on.

He moved Rosemary closer to him, pulling her tight with a strong arm muscled from shoveling coal, unbuttoned her flannel shirt and slid his hand inside covering the firm young breast. His fingers moved gently over the smooth skin and he felt the roughness of his own hand, his fingers picked and blistered from the shovel handle with black coal dirt ground into the nailbeds and into the creases no matter how hard he scrubbed with kerosene and Lava soap. He held his hand still. He might scratch her. He pulled the shirt-tail up and cradled her bare buttocks against his thighs, curving his legs under her. Wearing a flannel shirt for a nightgown had been his idea; it seemed better for a skinny young girl than the pink petticoat she had come shivering to bed in, and like to froze, the night they were married. He twisted his neck and peered at the Big Ben on the windowsill. Not yet three o'clock. Too early to wake her but he could not tolerate the bed and her nearness longer. He moved away carefully, tucked the heavy quilt against her back where he had been, leaving her warm.

The child began to cough as Ike pulled on his long johns and reached for his pants. She lay on a small cot against the wall, his Lisa. The quilt on her bed was of bright squares, yellow like sunshine and fruit orange and the white of angel wings, Lettie had said. Lettie wouldn't use an old quilt for filling for Lisa like she did the one he had just slipped out from under; instead she'd ordered new cotton batting from MacGruder down at the company store. She had filled the squares with the soft battling then tacked it with red string, softer, warmer, the best for Lisa. But Lettie would do anything for the child and when the fever came Lettie had worn herself out tending Lisa, pulled herself too low. When Lettie came down with the sore throat, he'd never thought it serious enough to call the Doctor - - not until it was too late.

He opened the stove door and threw in a shovel-full of coal; the fire flared up as the bug dust caught and he shut the door on the sulfur smell and yellow smoke. He whistled softly under his breath . . . Rise bullies, get your four o'clock coffee . . . He sat a small, enameled pot on the back of the stove and added coffee to the water to let it slow boil. Trouble was, Rosemary and the Doctor didn't understand how hard it was to pull up roots. He'd never thought of going to Florida, he'd never planned to leave here.

The child coughed again. He stood and looked down at her, the tiny face half-hidden under the quilt, the fair hair so like Lettie's, so small she hardly made a hump: the bed might just as well have been empty. Above her head the wind whistled through a crack in the wooden window frame. He found Lettie's sewing basket, setting where it always set, and took a ball of rag strips to the window. Using his pocketknife, he worked the cotton strip into the crack, packing it tight, then cut it off with his knife. Lettie would have started a rag rug when the ball got this big, hooking it at night while she waited for him to come home from the mine. He had yet to figure out what Rosemary did with her time – except draw pictures for Lisa. In the light from the stove he looked at the pictures flour-pasted on the wall, bright happy pictures of flowers and bees. He marveled at how real Rosemary had drawn the woods-violets, showing each petal curl, and it was easy to see this one was Dogwood in the spring; it reminded him of Lettie but he didn't tell that to Rosemary or to Lisa. It was easier not to talk about Lettie. One picture was of a funny clown and it had his name on it and music notes coming out of his mouth because he was forever whistling. "That's you, Pa," Lisa had said, then laughed so hard she began coughing, choking, and Rosemary had said again, "Please, Ike? Florida?" Lisa had seemed smaller, weaker, after that and so it was settled. Florida. He peeled the pictures off the wall carefully, placed them in the bottom of a pasteboard box and began packing dishes on top of them. Lisa would want her pictures wherever they went.

He kept the light out of the sleeping faces, was careful not to rattle the pots and pans. Once he stopped to drink a cup of strong coffee. Rosemary didn't know how much there was to do, to get ready to move; she thought they could do it all in the morning but he figured on leaving at daylight to get out of the mountains on the first day, not be caught in the hills after dark.

He filled the beanpot with water and set it on the stove to heat. Rosemary would sponge bathe herself and Lisa; they primped together like two girls the same age. Six and sixteen. Sometimes not much difference between them. But then, on the other hand . . . the beanpot. It reminded him. The day he had decided to marry Rosemary she had cooked beans in that pot for him the first time. She'd been good to stay with Lisa after Lettie died; he had paid her mighty little, but she kept the house clean and watched his girl. On the first cold morning, when frost lay like early snow on the brown garden-patch, touching the few collard greens and a single cabbage head that had burst open before it could be used and now was pecking greens for the wild chickens that roamed along the edge of the coal camp. On that first cold morning, Rosemary had burst through the door, bright-eyed, cheery-like, and she had shouted, "Mr. Ike, I'll cook you some beans today!"

"God, Rosemary, you can't cook beans to suit me—nobody can!" The beans had cooked slow all day in the iron pot on the back of the stove until the water turned thick and right for spooning over fried cornbread and sweet onions. When he had praised her, she'd looked straight into his dark, soot-rimmed eyes, not smiling, but soft and woman-old and he had seen the caring. "I'm old enough to know my mind," she'd said, and he had let the loneliness rise up, not stopping it this time but giving in to the hurting inside, letting go all the dark hours when he had lain under the patchwork quilt, alone with the emptiness, dry-eyed from needing Lettie.

"I'll speak to your Ma."

"I already told her," she'd said.

His two girls, he called them now, and Rosemary would not have guessed how he had come to feel about her, the lightness she brought, making it daytime even when it was dark outside before he got out of the mine. She'd given him back the whistling in a few short weeks.

29

He stood at the window and looked out, his packing nearly finished. One small light glowed against the dark hillside some distance away, like a misplaced star, and it made the mountains seem that much larger, leaning over him, holding him close, nourishing him in the darkness. He lived with that darkness, going down the long tunnel humped over in small cars through wind and cold and blackness in thick miners' clothes, black-crusted and stiff. That single light across the way hung from the north corner of the washhouse. It was always lit and a comfort to the men coming out. He stooped to the boxes again, stacking them beside the door ready for loading: it would be hard to move away.

Before daylight he was ready to tie the mattresses on top of the old car but Rosemary and Lisa slept on. He padded out to the back porch in his heavy woolen socks and pulled his miner's boots out from under the washstand. From a hook on the wall he took a heavy plaid mackinaw and quietly unlatched the screen door. He whistled softly to himself . . . in a cavern, in a canyon, excavating for a mine, dwelt a miner, forty-niner, and his daughter, Clementine. . . .

The road through the coal camp was deserted at this hour; his boots made crunching sounds on the frost-covered board walk. He moved onto the cindered road, followed it to the end of the row of houses, two-roomed, unpainted, identical wooden houses, and along the path at the edge of the wood. There the trees stood white-barked and still; the birds began to move about, not yet chirping for it was too early, a movement of wings, more felt than heard, and the dead leaves on the path took away the sound of his footsteps. He brushed past brown stick weeds, past fish-shaped milkweed pods hanging silvered and spent, past dried blackberry vines and old-red poison ivy twined on rot-slanted fence posts, and came to the river.

He stopped at the water's edge, listened to the soft flow of water and let the stillness fill him. He breathed in the cold air, lifted his head and looked at the black mountains touched by the blue dawn light, pulled back his shoulders and stood straight . . . on a hill far away. . . .

Whistling softly, he waded into the clear shallows to a large flat gray rock and ran his hand through the cold mountain water, feeling along the underside of the rock. Gray lichens flaked off the rock as he pulled a trot line out of the water, caught the strings attached and carefully drew in two gray-green bass and a mud-brown horny-head. He slipped them free of the hooks, pulled a piece of tarp out of his pocket, rolled the fish into it while they were still flopping. He drew out a Prince Albert can filled with fresh bait and then stopped: no one would be here to take the fish off tomorrow. There was no use baiting the hooks. He dropped the tobacco can back into his pocket and let the line go; it slipped under the rock, out of sight. He left the river whistling softly, . . . oh my darlin', oh my darlin' oh my darlin,' Clementine. . . .

By the time he got back to the house the light was better, fine for cleaning fish; he scaled the bass beside the back hog- wire fence, chuckling as two spotted dogs came out from under the house and started fighting over the entrails. He threw the loser the horny head which he didn't bother to clean.

He laid the bass on the wash bench and removed his boots. In a moment he had lard melted and hot in an iron skillet and a batter of cornmeal and water to roll the fish in, four flat pieces, one each for his girls, and two for himself. The cornmeal sizzled and popped, and covering the handle with a rag, he lifted the skillet to let the grease cool. He began his morning song, anxious to hear Lisa's small laugh and Rosemary's mock dismay . . . rise, bullies, get your four o'clock coffee, stable boss is up and he's done his work, now it's time to call the commissary clerk, rise bullies, get your four o'clock coffee. . . .

"It's not four o'clock, Pa."

"How do you know, littlun?"

"It never is when you sing that."

31

"This time it's mighty close to it."

He flipped the fish in the pan and set it off the stove. The heat from the heavy cast iron pan would finish cooking it.

He sat on the bed beside Rosemary, feeling the warmth of her neck on his hand. "I've been thinking," he said. She looked at him, waiting in silence for him to continue, small-curled beneath the heavy quilt.

"We can go to the ocean on Sundays. You can have your pick of the Atlantic or the Gulf of Mexico."

Her answering smile made him want to get in the warm bed with her, touch her and feel the joy pour out of her and pass into him as it did each time, but because it was dawn and because they had a long way to go, he reached for her jeans instead, handing them to her, knowing she would dress under the covers to keep warm.

"Fish are done," he said, . . . rise bullies, get your four o'clock coffee. . .."

Evan after his early packing it took half of the morning to load the car with what they were taking and more time to give away what was left. Rosemary filled a zinc bucket with water and mopped the worn linoleum.

"For God's Sake, Rosemary! We need to be on the road. The floor will just get dirty again!"

"I ain't leaving a dirty house, Ike!"

"But it's nearly noon! We'll never get over the mountains afore dark."

"I ain't leaving a dirty house."

She finished her mopping and threw the black water out the door, scattering the dogs.

The boxes were loaded, mattresses tied on top of the old car. Ike made a good bed for Lisa on top of a pile of clothes on the back seat of the car and covered her with her downy quilt.

Rosemary insisted they stop to see her Ma for it would be a long while before they would see her again. Ike sat in the front room and listened to the two women talking in the kitchen, knowing he could tell when Rosemary was ready to leave.

"Rosemary, I know you don't want to go –"

"But, Ma, I do want to go!"

"—but it's your duty, since you had to marry that man, if your Pa were alive—"

"I want to see Florida, and wear some of the new clothes, and smell the orange blossoms, and Ike says we can go the ocean on Sundays and - - -"

"You'll be homesick in a week."

"I'll have my own home Ma, and I have Lisa."

"It's a shame for you to be straddled with another woman's child, young as you are, and her a sick child at that."

"I love Lisa, Ma. It's like having a little sister, and Ike's good to me."

"Why wouldn't he be? Got a good cook and a babysitter fer nothin', didn't he?"

"Ma, we'll be leavin' now –"

"Not yet! Chicken is almost done and you got to eat somewhere, might as well be here."

Ike walked down to the company store after hearing that the chicken was not yet ready, with Lisa riding high on his shoulders. MacGruder stood in front of the store, flour-sack apron tied around his waist, spitting Brown Mule over the iron rail into the cindered roadbed. MacGruder did more than just clerk the store, he kept folks in touch, passed around the news. Most folks who moved away sent him back a picture postcard saying where they went and how they were doing. He tacked these on the wall beside the front door for everyone to read when they came in for staples or tobacco. As Ike and Lisa came up the stone steps he started talking.

"So yo're off to Florida, hey Ike?"

"Yep. Get Lisa some sunshine and oranges."

"Look up Fred Tate. He moved down there 'bout a year ago. Folks say he's doing well, runs one of them serve-yourself gas stations, don't do repairs, just pumps gas. Hardly gets his hands dirty all day long."

"I'll do that. I got his address off the wall. Might be he could put me on to something."

"Hear tell you never need a coat."

"That's what they say. I give my mackinaw away."

MacGruder threw the tobacco over the rail and shook his big head. "Should have kept it in the family—you'll be back. Ever'body comes back soon as they get a chance."

At the house people were gathered; Rosemary and Lisa were hugged and kissed around. Rosemary came to Ike with tears holding back and a tight chin. She looked old and she looked young and he could not be sure which would win out.

"We'll come back in the spring," he said, "we'll come back to visit with the first thaw."

He watched the worry flutter over her face and the sad draw out of her eyes like fog draws out of the valley at first sun and he wondered again at her belonging to him. He wrapped Lisa in her cloud-soft quilt and covered Rosemary with a shawl that had belonged to Lettie.

It was much later than he had meant to leave, what with the long meal and the good-byes, and it had started to snow. He slid his hand under the shawl and between her thighs and started whistling as he settled down to drive.... *Oh, my darlin', oh my darlin', oh, my darlin' Clementine. . ..*

Ike was bothered by the late start for he knew it would be dark early in the mountains, being November: the sun dropped behind the hills and the wind rose in icy swirls. He pushed steadily on, covering the miles as rapidly as the old car with its load could manage, winding into dusk-blued hills over frozen roads full of

34

chugholes. He persisted with his faint song, more humming than whistling . . .you are lost and gone forever..., the mountains folded one over another and icicles hung from gray rocks like beard on an old man's face. He drove through steep forests with great logs downed, lying rotting, moss-covered, turning white in the falling snow. The oak leaves clung tenaciously to dead branches, the dead leaves moving in the wind, while lesser trees had long ago let their leaves fall and were naked and bare.

Snow began to accumulate and stick to the road surface as he climbed higher into the hills. Rosemary began to sag beside him, talking only occasionally, dreaming again her favorite dream of seeing the ocean. "I can't swim, Ike." I'll teach you" "You can swim?" "Yep, learned in the river." "They say salt water is different." "Can't be much harder than swimmin' in the river."

In a short while Rosemary curled up in the seat beside him, her head cradled on her arm. He slipped his hand into the front of her shirt, needing to touch her, but she shrugged him away, not wanting to be kept awake. He began to feel her drowsiness and wanted to sleep with her and rubbed the back of his neck to keep awake. And continued to whistle. . . down in the valley, valley so low, hear the wind blow, love, hear the wind blow . . . .

The snow came thicker, faster, wind-driven in the car lights. He skidded on the curves as the wind caught under the mattresses tied on the top and he was forced to reduce his speed. The old car struggled to cross the steep slopes of Gauley Mountain and crept even slower on the icy downhill side. In the valley he drove a little faster, but ice had formed in patches and he couldn't see the water. . .. angels in heaven know I love you.

He put his arm over the back of the seat, trying to see if Lisa was covered up, but couldn't reach her, and topped the ridge, seeing scattered lights far below... know I love you, love, know I love you... "Hey, Lisa! Look down there! See those lights? That's not stars, Lisa, that's a town! Want to see a roller-coaster ride?" When Lisa did not answer, he turned to Rosemary. "Want some coffee? I sure to God could use a cup." But Rosemary didn't answer either. The headlights picked up on white posts and double cables of guard rails, swung back to the mountains—the mountain skinned halfway up when the road was built—sometimes picking out a lone scrub cedar sprouted hopeful-like in the crevice of gray rock. Occasionally an unpainted shack would seem to leap out from a curve, set on high stilts with its back against the hill, a snow-covered garden patch beside it . . . hear the wind blow, love, hear the wind blow . . . .

After some time, he reached the small town, deserted in the winter night, no one on the single icy street. By the time he skidded to a stop before a shabby eating place he was almost ill. On the front of the small café a naked light bulb hung over a small sign: Open All Night. He left the motor running to keep the car warm and ordered two cups of coffee and two cups of hot chocolate, taking long enough to drink one cup of coffee straight down while the old pudgy owner put the other three cups in a shoe box for easy carrying. He held the door for Ike against the wind. Ike eased into the car, set the shoe box on the dash and then, turning around, he tried to get Lisa to sit up. He moved the soft quilt away from her face and slipped one hand under her head, raising her from the car seat.

"Lisa? Lisa!"

"God! Rosemary!"

The hot chocolate spilled over the bright comforter as he grabbed the child by both hands. A dark stain spread over the white squares. "Rosemary! Help me Help me!"

He looked at the small, still face, laid her back in the seat and ran to the café.

"Get me a doctor! Hurry, Hurry!"

"No phone."

"Where's the closest one?"

"Take her to the hospital —there's a nurse there—she'll get the doctor for you."

"Which way?"

"Left at the corner, two blocks; you can't miss it!"

Ike ran back to the car, pray, pray something, but he had already prayed, that morning, by the river.

The small hospital was soot-stained red brick, saturated with years of soft coal dust and smoke, but the windows reflected the lights as he swung the car into the ambulance entrance, flung the door open and grabbed Lisa wrapped tightly in her special quilt. An old negro orderly in a white starched jacket braced the door, holding it as the wind pushed them inside.

"Come in, Sir! Come right in!"

Ike blinked in the sterile glare of fluorescent lighting, stood uncertainly in the entranceway. A young, red-haired nurse took his arm and guided him into a room. He laid the child on the examining table and stared at her face. The nurse pushed him away abruptly.

"Jackson!"

The elderly negro shuffled to the door. The nurse was removing the bright quilt and loosening Lisa's coat.

"Get Kincaid! Quick!"

"Yes, Miss Margie, Right away!" Jackson hurried from the room, mumbling, "And de Doctor ten miles away."

Margie thumped the child sharply on the chest, slipped an airway into place and began breathing, push, breath, push, breath. . ..

Almost instantly an older Nurses' Aide appeared in the doorway. She was older, short and thin, in a white uniform and run-down shoes. She kicked the shoes off, hopped up on a metal footstool to the examining table, knelt beside the child and began heart massage, push, up, push, . . . on a hill far away, push, push, up, breathe, Ike stood motionless in a sea of motion as the two nurses worked together, their rhythm as regular as the waves, push, relax, breathe. . .stood an old rugged cross. . .

37

He watched the wrinkled substantial hands of Kincaid as she pressed, released, pressed with hope, released with resignation, press, release, press, release, her small wrinkled face showing the strain, lips together, perspiration forming at the edges of her short gray-brown hair, clear-edged glasses slipping down on her nose. . . rise bullies . . . showing the strain.

Margie's young strong arms moved on the black ambu bag, in, out, in, out, now surreptitiously feeling for a pulse at the tiny throat, her face serious, flushed with exertion, red hair swinging as she leaned forward, white cap thrown on the shelf in the corner cabinet, in, out, get your four o'clock coffee. . . it's not four o'clock, Daddy, . . . it never is. . .

Ike spoke hesitantly, "Rosemary ...." Old Jackson interrupted, "Doctor comin' soon." Margie interrupted, "Here, Jackson, take this, quickly! Let me get a stimulant." Margie stepped to the medicine cabinet and Jackson took the ambu bag, his strong black hands picked up the rhythm as he joined Kincaid, push, push, breathe. . .. oh, my darlin', oh, my darlin'. . .

Ike's rough hands moved over his short denim jacket, searching for the pockets, and not finding them, hung loose and empty at his sides . . . dreadful sorry, clementine. . .. A large, flat-faced clock was built into the wall over the sink; He followed the nurses' eyes. Five-forty. Less than four hours from home.

Margie and Kincaid changed places, never breaking the rhythm, press, release, breathe, silence moved into the room. He felt the loneliness beginning again, like before, remembered. His hands found the jacket pockets and crept inside. He would go home for the healing, back to the hills . . . on a hill far away, stood an old rugged cross. . . I will lift up my eyes to the hills. . .. The nurses stopped and looked at him, waiting, the young one crying. . . hear the wind blow, love . . . he looked at the flat clock and counted the minutes in disbelief. He felt the cold wind, like when he was inside the mine, only it was colder now, darker. . .. hear the wind blow . . .

"It was too damned cold to roll down the window," he said. His eyes moved to the glass door, to the waiting car, wanting to go out, not wanting to go out, knowing and not knowing . . ..

He turned back to the nurses. "Rosemary is in the car," he said.

He did not follow as they rushed out into the night.

TWO

END OF A SUMMER DAY

A goose-pimpled boy with teeth so white
Chattering, shivering in fading light,
Wet trunks clinging to brown skin tight,
Saying, "Mom, please, let's stay 'til night."

A red-headed tot with suntan for Cape,
Pink suit rounding a tiny fat shape,
Wet sand patted in a fine fat cake
Saying, "Mom, please, it's not so late."

A sun-haired girl with a winning smile
And childish charms young for guile,
With blistered nose joining the file,
Saying, "Mom, please, wait a while."

~Betty Roberts

Stump Dreams
Oil on Canvas by Betty Roberts

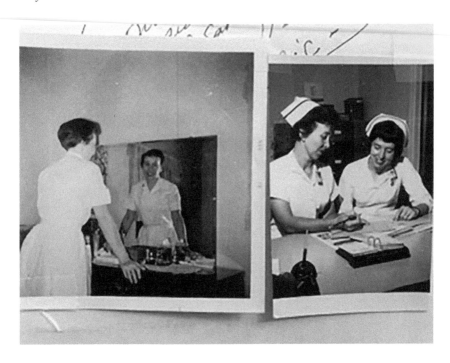

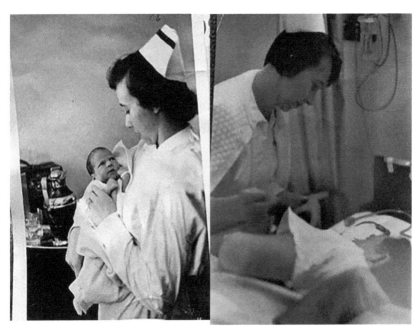

Nursing pictures of Betty Osborne

After graduation, my husband took the children and I with him on a job-seeking trip to the south. We left West Virginia in a snow storm, late in the evening, the four children put to bed in the back of a nearly-new gray Mercury station wagon, so big it held a regular- sized mattress, with a wooden box strapped on top for the luggage.

By six a.m. we were in Georgia, warm breeze, the scent of flowers, and four starving kids. We stopped at a "Mom & Pop's" diner for breakfast. Conscious of our very meager budget, I ordered scrambled eggs and toast for all of them, their Dad and I being still tanked up from all the coffee we had brought with us to drink while driving.

When the plates were served, the eggs were nearly covered with thick cream of wheat.

"I didn't order cream of wheat," I said to the waitress, an older woman in a sunshine yellow apron.

"Why, Honey, that ain't cream of wheat! Them's grits and they are free, comes with the meal! Ain't you never seen grits? You must be a Yankee!"

I thought about my history lessons: West Virginia was the only state ever formed from within another state. It was during the war between the north and the south and W.V. seceded from Virginia over the question of slavery. No doubt about it, we were in the South! The children tasted the grits and turned up their noses. "You put butter on them," the waitress said. They tried that and still wouldn't eat the grits. "Put sugar on them," I said," like you do cream of wheat."

The waitress put her hands on her hips and tossed her head. "Humph! You don't put sugar on grits!" But the kids ate every bite of their first grits—with sugar.

After breakfast we drove a short distance and took a slight detour to let the children and I see the ocean. It was a bright, warm day, a surprise to us as February in our home state was the middle of winter, with snow and cold temperatures. My husband saw several cars driving along the beach and there were no signs forbidding it. He parked in a few minutes and the children removed their shoes and socks and headed for the waves coming up across the sand. I couldn't resist and soon joined them. We walked along the shore, collected shells and driftwood, watched the sand crabs run for cover, and the gulls diving for them. Before we were ready, my husband called to us; we still had several hours to go before reaching his sister's home in Florida. Regretfully, we got back in the car, sand and all.

He started the car, put it in gear, and nothing happened. The wheels spun, throwing wet sand behind them, digging into a hole. The heavily loaded station wagon was stuck. It was not until then that I noticed the tide had come in and the car was sitting in several inches of water.

My husband got out of the car, walked around it, came back and opened the doors. "Better get out, lighten the load. I'll try it again." About this time, we heard the noise of a machine coming up behind us. An old man in blue overalls and a straw hat sat on a rusty, old tractor. He also wore a wide grin. "You folks got a little trouble?"

My husband walked back to greet him, relief evident on his face. That expression changed as the old man said, "Pull you out. No problem."

"How much?" my husband asked.

"Hundred dollars," he drawled.

My husband hesitated. The old man took his hat off, scratched his head, and waited, watching the children as they once again splashed in the water which was rapidly rising around the automobile. "All these your'en?" he asked. My husband replied, "Sure are."

"First time been to the ocean?"

"First time," my husband said. I wanted him to be more friendly, more talkative to the old man, but he just stood there, waiting for the old man to do the talking. In a few minutes, both of them watching the children, the old man said, "Well, a hundred is my standard but I've already made my day. Reckon I can get you out for fifty." Then, my husband grinned, reached out a friendly hand, and thanked him. They talked for a few more minutes, and the old man said that he made his living on the "Dumb Yankees" who never bothered to find out when the tide came in. He pulled a heavy chain out of the box on his tractor, and in less than ten minutes he had the loaded car on dry ground, the children wiped the sand off and put their shoes on. For the next hour all we heard was, "I'm hungry—when are we stopping again?" But very conscious of our limited funds, our next meal was at Aunt Frances's house, in Florida.

After a couple of days in the Sanford-Orlando area, where he put in applications at the colleges, we drove to Mississippi, on the Gulf coast. His younger sister had married a West Virginia boy who had enlisted in the Air Force and was stationed at Kessler Air Force Base. He immediately told us that the Air Force was hiring teachers and my husband wasted no time putting in an application. The next day he was called for an interview and our brother-in-law went to the Air Base with him. He was hired immediately. When he told me he would be teaching electronics, I said, "You don't know anything about electronics!" He replied, with a confident grin, "But I can learn. It can't be much harder than electricity."

We drove back to West Virginia, packed up a large U-Haul, loading it while it snowed, and moved to the Gulf Coast, renting a house one block from the beach, halfway between Kessler Air Force Base and Gulfport. The next day, I went to Gulfport Memorial Hospital and had a job interview. With my experience, a place in Delivery room was offered immediately.

We loved living on the Gulf Coast, only one block off the beach, pines and palms, magnificent old oaks with their evergreen leaves on long branches reaching nearly to the ground, very different from our mountains covered with hardwood trees turning brilliant colors in the fall, just before shedding them to stand naked and bare through the winter. Here, even in February, everything was green, green, green.

BUDDY-BOY

He didn't know no better," Sister said, apology oozing in her voice like always when she talked about Buddy-Boy, and I couldn't help but giggle. Sister looked at me real sharp, and of course I hushed, always do when she looks at me slant-eyed mean.

"He ain't but eleven," she said, and Mama nodded. "Eleven's knows better!"

Buddy-Boy slunk down, hands in his jean's pockets, dark head barely level with the back of the old church pew, red and white T-shirt standing out bright against the dark wood, Coca-Cola in white letters across the front. He had such a grin, Buddy-Boy did, a little sneaky but mostly pure fun, bright for his age, learned to read before five, looking over my shoulder, too bright, Aunt Margaret said, always in trouble.

"He don't know how to b'have at funerals," I said, "No more'n I do."

"Best you both learn," Mama, said "and that right fast. Sit up, Buddy-Boy, now sit up stiff and still!"

The Preacher arose, moved before the choir as they began to moan, Jesus, Jesus, ah, sweet Jesus. Uncle Matthew lay in a steel gray coffin, bald head shining like an old tobacco stain against an ivory pillow, gray beard fresh-clipped and combed.

Everybody was here, some from as far as Selma and Birmingham, where we lived before coming to Arkadelphia.

Great-Aunt Pricilla was sleeping in Buddy-Boy's room and daughter Lila had piled in with us in spite of Sister's objections. Not that I minded company—Buddy-Boy and I had friends over all the time—but Sister, she didn't want some old maid cousin sharing her room, pilfering through her chiff-a-robe, looking for Lord knows what. Even mama don't do that, respects our privacy, she says, but, frankly, I think she's skeered of what she'd find, maybe Sister's cigarettes and she'd have to haul her up short. We don't tell Mama everything, only Buddy-Boy knows everything, and he'd no more tell than Sister and I'd tell on him when he sneaks out middle of the night and goes crawdabbin' and froggin'.

The Preacher was standing and praising, everybody crying, and the noise was rising louder and louder, couldn't half hear what Buddy-Boy was whispering, something about going , and I know Mama couldn't hear him—she's been half deaf for years, her hearing ruined by the racket of the sewing machines down at the shirt factory. Mama , she's fond of saying she's sewed a seam'd go round the world , and I'd say, if it goes round the world, it is back, and Mama'd say, Hush your mouth, Norma Jean you know what I mean, if'n yore Pa was livin' he'd take some of that smart out of you! Mama, she really did try and she didn't want to know every single little thing Buddy-Boy and I do, she's got her hands full keeping taters on the table, she says.

Folks on the other side filing by now, taking a long last look, and Buddy-boy, slipping behind me, eased into the line, and if Mama even noted she didn't call him back. Before we knowed it, he was gone. Out the back door and flying down the road to the swimming hole and how I wished I could fly with him! Stuck between mama and Great-Aunt Pricilla, trying to act like a lady, now, if I put my nose in the air, lighten my hair the way she's done—straightened and red—or maybe more make-up, heavier on the rouge, it'd show up better on me, more yellow in my skin, Sister says, lighter, I say.

Uncle Matthew's widow, Aunt Margaret, she's hanging on to the casket now, she's carrying on right good. Pity she hadn't done a little more while Uncle Matt was alive. He treated us good, me and Buddy-Boy—especially Buddy-boy him not having any kids, treated him like a son.

The way Aunt Margaret's crying reminds me of the cat—she carried on just like that when Buddy-Boy found Uncle Matt's old razor and finding it was an accomplishment, considering Aunt Margaret's house, old clothes piled around, sack after sack of aluminum cans, Uncle Matt's collection, worth money, he'd say. Said, "Soon as I git to feelin' better, you, me and Buddy-boy, we'll take 'em in, go down to the Rexall fer a soder pop. We'll all three go," he'd say, knowing Buddy-Boy had picked up most of those cans all by himself to help Uncle Matt out, him being old and weak.

The choir was singing Beautiful River, Old Rugged Cross, River Jordan, on and on and on. About the cat, Aunt Margaret blamed me 'stead of Buddy-Boy, said I shoulda knowed better, and I did. That razor worked really well on the cat's sides, just got raggedy on the tail. Uncle Matt had laughed, laughed until he started coughing. Aunt Margaret said that's what brought on the hemorrhage, but Uncle Matt, he said it didn't matter, had to go sometime and he'd rather die laughing, took Buddy-Boy on the bed beside him and hugged him hard, Buddy-Boy grinning ear to ear, Lord! How Uncle Matt loved that boy!

Now the preacher was praying, kneeling beside the communion rail, sound coming muffled like under water. Not that Aunt Margaret didn't love Buddy-Boy. She did, practically raised him after Pa died, what with me and Sister in school and Mama working, and she cooked up flapjacks with Yellow-label syrup for him and Uncle Matt, their favorite.

Now our side can view, and Mama didn't faint from the smell—and the memory when she passed the carnations. She did when Papa died, and Buddy-Boy had dumped the flower water on her to revive her, something none of the grown-ups thought to do. Some of them were real upset with Buddy-Boy, Mama's good dress all wet, you know, but Uncle Matt, he took a holt of Buddy-Boy and says, nobody'll touch this boy while I'm alive! Lord, don't seem real, Uncle Matt gone: who will look after Buddy-Boy now?

The ushers, neighboring men looking something in suits and ties, and Sister's eyeing them real careful, husband-hunting, more'n likely, seeing which one'd look good at a wedding. They roll that casket right easy, don't look heavy at all, and there's flowers for Sister, Lila, and me —I could carry two, I'm so tall. Willowy. That's what Uncle Matt called me. Me and buddy-Boy was scuffling. Aunt Margaret pulling at us, called me ugly and Uncle Matt said, "Well she mought be ugly now, but you wait a few years, them long legs, she'll be right willowy. You wait and see!"

Well, Uncle Matt. Sure glad you lived to see me all growed up, taller than Sister was at sixteen, some say prettier, too. Wish you could 'a waited longer. On account of Buddy-Boy; he ain't found himself yet.

That's one deep hole in the ground, they're setting that casket down right careful like. Poor Aunt Margaret, looks so small all of a sudden 'tween Mama and Great-Aunt Pricilla, she'll be so lost with Uncle Matt gone, 'course, if Buddy-Boy stays with her, like Mama said he could, now that'll keep her busy washing blue jeans and cleaning up behind him —if he was here right now, he'd have this red mud all over him! Mama's going to be mad when she figures out he's gone.

Big crowd today, some outside the fence, and this cemetery is bigger than most, dates back to slave days, Mama says, and our ancestors are buried right here, before the land was private owned.

Those men, down by the creek there, what'er they doin'? Don't look like they are here for the funeral, coming up the hill, most of 'em are white, a uniform or two.

"Which one is Mary Lewis?"

"I'm Mary Lewis." *Mama steps forward.*

"Ma'am, we hate to interrupt, service and all, but, uh, we think, ah, --"

"What is it? What are you saying"?

"Could you come with us? We think it's your boy —"

"My boy? Buddy-Boy? What's he done now?"

Down by the creek a crowd had collected. Someone shouted, "What's going on?"

"Little nigger boy —done drowned hisself!"

Oh, God! Lord, Lord, Oh, Lord!" The cries went up, Mama, she went down. Fainted. Like she done when Papa died. But no Buddy-Boy to bring her 'round.

"Norma Jean," *Sister was saying,* "You go see. I'll take ker'a Mama."

I went down to the creek, following the men, one a deputy, gun butt hittin' agin his leg, pop, pop, pop, and the ground dry, red dust puffs around his shoes and I matched my steps with his and we walked down the hill, my legs near as long as his. And there was one, a white man, pulled out his handkerchief, handed it to me, "Case you need it," *he said, and why would I need it, he was the one sweatin'.*

Somebody'd put a towel over him, laying there on the red clay bank, and only his feet stuck out, and the deputy started to lift the towel but another man said, "never mind, I don't need to see him, he used to come in the store with Matthew, she don't need to see." *The white man took my elbow, looked straight into my eyes and said,* "You all right, Sister?" *and I —I jerked my arm away.* "She's Sister, "I said, nodding my head toward the church. "I'm Norma Jean." *And I gave him his handkerchief back too.*

The next two days you couldn't tell who took it harder, mama or Aunt Margaret. Sister cried all the first day, leaving Great-Aunt Pricilla, Lila and me to do all the work, folks stayed, too far to make two trips 'specially for those from Selma, and they made extra cooking.

Not much difference in funerals, casket, flowers, preachin', crying and carrying on, but if anything, there were more folks at Buddy's funeral more white folks, too, mostly saying, well, Matt had a good long life, but Buddy-Boy, he shoulda had a few more years, a little more time. It was hot, crowded, damn carnations smellin' worse than ever and frankly, I was glad when it was over. I never did cry.

We came home alone, Mama, Sister and me. Great-Aunt Pricilla and Lila took Aunt Margaret home with them to Selma, said it wasn't good for her to stay alone, we had each other. Sister was almost faint, crying all the time. And the heat had dried her out, Mama said. And Mama herself didn't look too good. I made them tea in tall glasses, poured it over ice and cut a lemon, put a yellow slice over the edge of the glasses like in the magazines, making it look cool and special. Carried it out to them on a tin tray, out to the porch swing where mama and Sister sat together.

"Here, Mama, drink this—it'll do you good, and Sister, here's yours - - -Ah-h-h-h-h! Oh, God! O, God!"

"Why'd you fix four, Norma Jean?" Mama said, "Why'd you make four glasses of tea?"

I'll never forget my first evening on duty at Gulfport, Mississippi. Our supper, in the main dining room, was a part of our income, and it being 'free', I skipped down to the main floor to eat with other staff members. Served cafeteria style, I pushed my tray along the rail until I came to the vegetables. A large, black woman was serving, and I asked for the spinach. "No spinach, honey-chile," she replied. "What is that green stuff?" I asked. "Them's turnip greens," she said. "What's that white stuff in them?"

"White stuff? White stuff? Oh, you mean the roots?"

"You cook the roots in the greens? "I asked, amazed.

"Why, shore! Don't nothing go to waste! Where yo from— you must be a Yankee!"

"West Virginia," I replied." We let the roots grow big, make turnips!"

The next stainless-steel pan held black-eyed peas, which I recognized. The sight of those peas reminded me of another favorite family story.

When I was eight years old, Mother and Dad took us to New York, to the World's Fair. We obtained passes on the Pullman since my father was a railroad employee, and we three girls shared a bunk at night. It was very exciting, with many new and strange sights, one of which was my first encounter with a black man. The dining car butler, an older, dignified man, dressed in a black tuxedo, stiff white shirt and black bow tie, complete with a snowy white towel over his arm, took our order for dinner. Mother ordered for all of us, and when our plates were served there was a strange, new bean on them. They were brown, like our pinto beans, but they had a black spot on them! I thought they got that way because it was a black man serving them! We all ate them; thought they were delicious. Back home again, Mother bought black-eyed peas for the first time, since we had raved about them on the train. Neither of her three daughters would eat them, Dad said he'd rather have pintos, so she never cooked them again.

Moving to Mississippi had been something of a shock to me, so far from home, requiring more than a weekend off work to make the trip back, and with our schedules, we were unable to go unless it was a holiday with extra days off. I struggled with homesickness, missing my Mom and Dad, and the farm, and in those days calling on the phone was only for emergencies. My parents' phone had been installed after the railroad pressured the phone company to put the line in especially for Dad because he was on 24-hour call for emergencies on the railroad. Calling just to "chat" was something we didn't do. My Mom had read some of my stories over the years, and now, living so far away, she loved for me to mail a copy of what I was writing for her to read. When she got one of my stories, she would read it aloud to my Dad, involving him in the process. During this time, my younger sister was still at home, in high school, and she expressed an interest also.

Mom became interested and started sending me what she was writing. We felt cheated when we got a letter and it didn't have some bit of "creative writing" included. At one time, Mom sent a manuscript about her duties as the wife of a railroader, and what she sent, written in long hand, with a pencil, became a part of the material I always carried with me every time we moved. While planning this Chronicle, I told my daughter and my sisters about having the story, written in her handwriting so long ago. Her manuscript is included here, for the benefit of all the children, mine, and my sister's families. Unfortunately, Mom didn't do anything with what she wrote, and after we made the next move, we were close enough to go home more frequently. Writing letters wasn't quite so important. Could it be, maybe I had grown up a bit and no longer got so homesick?

This original story was written by mother, Grace Etta Jackson Phipps, and has been included in the volume of short stories as a memorial to her and to my father, Wallace Bryant Phipps, the "railroader" she wrote about.

Dad spent his entire working years as a lineman on a railroad, beginning as a water boy at the age of eight. In 1928, he transferred from the Norfolk and Western Railroad to the

Virginian and moved up to foreman with his own motor car and crew. His career spanned the steam engine, then to the electric engine when it was invented and ended with the change from the electric to the diesel.

This is a true story and is copied from her handwritten pages.

THE EXPERIENCES OF A RAILROADER'S WIFE

I've been working for the railroad thirty-four years now, yet I've never been on the payroll. There must be hundreds of workers in the same category as myself, but we are never recognized by the railroad executives. Why? I'll tell you why. They consider the job to be so insignificant it doesn't merit any recognition, yet there have been times when movement in the entire area was at a stand-still and I, personally, did my bit to get it going again.

I became a railroad worker in 1927, when I married into the railroad family. My husband and I set up housekeeping in a six-room cottage in an abandoned mining camp. The house was comfortable, nice, as compared to the scores of vacant houses surrounding it. Our closest neighbor was a quarter mile away, but with rows and rows of vacant houses the isolation was not keenly felt. It was during the "lean years", just preceding the depression, when men were hunting jobs all over the nation. We wouldn't have chosen this desolate place to begin our life together, but since we had no choice in the matter, we were happy to be counted among the fortunate few who had jobs.

The Virginian was a coal-hauling railroad and ran through a remote section of the country, winding through the mountains of West Virginia. The system was electrified, and my husband was foreman of one of the line gangs which maintained the catenary system. It meant that he was subject to call. Any time there was a power failure anywhere in his territory, or quite often in either of the four sections, he worked around the clock until the train movement was restored. As a consequence, I was frequently alone at home at night.

Fortunately, my husband realized the possible danger under these circumstances, and he provided a rifle, a shot gun and a pistol for our protection. We went in for target practice until I could stand on my front porch and kill a squirrel by shooting it in the head at a distance of fifty yards. His foresight paid off earlier than expected.

One night he was called out to work around eleven o'clock for an emergency. I have never been able to sleep at night when he is working, and early in our marriage I had formed the habit of sewing, doing needlework, or reading during his absence. I had been doing handwork for a couple of hours when I heard footsteps stealthily crossing the front porch of the house. I knew the sound was not that of my husband's sprightly walk. Then, I thought, maybe he was teasing me.

I went noiselessly toward the door but before I reached it, I saw the door knob slowing turning. I took two steps back through the French doors into the dining room and got the sixteen-gauge pump gun from the rack. I loaded the chamber and spoke my husband's name, saying "I've got a gun! If it is you, speak to me, otherwise I am going to shoot!". For an answer there was a lunge against the door. I pointed the gun at the bottom of the door and pulled the trigger. The prowler ran, and I heard him falling down the long flight of stairs at the end of the porch in his hasty departure. I didn't have to worry about him anymore!

The railroad company had installed a telephone in our house in order to call my husband at all hours of the night and at short notice. It was not an ordinary phone, but one of thousands hooked up along the line and was for railroad business only. By pushing the little black button, one could hear conversations all up and down the line, and by pushing the little black button, you could join in the conversation.

I had been instructed in the use of the phone and felt free to use it anytime it was necessary. This was a privilege extended to me for all the help I gave them from time to time.

Although my husband was not paid extra for all the additional hours he worked above the eight-hour day, for nearly a quarter of a century some member of the family had to stay in hearing distance all times of the day or night.

Someone had to find him, and that someone was usually me. One evening he had gone squirrel hunting on the mountain back of the house. When the phone rang, I took the shotgun outside and fired three shots in rapid succession. In three minutes flat he was home and started for headquarters.

It was a rare occasion when he got permission to be away and at those times a relief man stood in readiness. It was a rule of the company that a line gang foreman was allowed thirty minutes to get the crew together, line up their equipment and get their instructions from the power director and be ready to proceed to the trouble spot. This was exceedingly difficult when you consider that each of the six men were scattered in all directions. Often it was necessary for me to lend a hand by rounding up the gang while my husband got train orders, checked equipment and took care of all the details related to the job at hand.

Needless to say, there was never any time for food before leaving for the trouble area. Many times, a meal was prepared, even the family seated for a special occasion such as a birthday celebration but always the job came first. I remember one time in particular, a guest remarked that he would not have a job that was that demanding. At that time, the guest had been unemployed for two years.

When my husband was called out, the time varied, from an hour to thirty-six hours. I have known him to work around the *clock three times without a break. The crew under him would be replaced for a rest period but there was not a relief supervisor to direct the replacements. It was not unusual for these men to work all day, then within an hour be called out for an emergency, work all night, then report for work the next day right on schedule as usual.*

For years I've been listening in on the telephone hoping to hear my husband's voice when he reported into the dispatcher. Often, I waited anxiously for his return, hoping to learn when he would be ready to return home so that I could have hot food ready without unnecessary delay. I learned to figure almost to the quarter hour when to expect him by listening to his report when he energized the line. The trains couldn't run until he called in to the P.D. that the lines were hot again.

I remember one time in particular when he didn't get home at the regular time. One of our children got sick during the day. Her temperature went up several degrees during the afternoon and I planned to take her to the doctor in the evening when my husband got home so that I could use the car as the doctor was nine miles away.

I tried home remedies, cool sponge baths, doses of aspirin but neither seemed to help. Finally, I put a hot water bottle under her head, and she settled into a restless sleep. I sat by her bed all night; I couldn't leave the other two children, aged one and five to walk five miles to headquarters to get the car and no one lived in calling distance. The railroad phone was my only means of communication. I went to the phone and called the P.D. When I lifted the receiver, I recognized my husband's voice. He was on his way home. I sat down and cried with relief.

One day there was a knock on the door and when I answered there was a large dirty man standing before me. He asked for food, and I closed the door behind me, went to the kitchen and put a bottle of milk in a brown paper bag, added a loaf of bread and jar of homemade strawberry jam and brought it back to the door. The man was leering at me with the most horrifying expression it had ever been my experience to witness. His evil, gloating expression took me by surprise. At first, I didn't understand his intent and held out the bag to him. He didn't take it, only stood there with that evil grin. Suddenly, realizing my danger, I knew I must not panic.

He was a huge man and I was certain I would be helpless in his grasp. I knew too that I must not let him know how frightened I was or that I was alone in the house. I stood, holding the bag out to him for what seemed like ages. I was positive that I could not get back in the house before he could catch me. Then I heard a low growl from the bottom of the steps. Old Bouncer was so gentle he had never shown any signs of aggression and I doubt very much if he would have harmed even this character. But it was my only hope. I said, "Hold it boy!" I sat the bag of food down and went down the steps and got hold of Bouncer's collar. "If you are hungry, you take that bag of food and get out of here before I turn this dog loose on you!" He did just that, running down the steps, and on down the driveway. If he had not been so scared of dogs, he might have noticed that Old Bouncer was happily wagging his tail the entire time!

After living in Mississippi for two years, my husband transferred to Huntsville, Alabama, trading the airmen for soldiers and received a raise in civil service grade. He quickly learned the Nike Hercules missile system and taught the soldiers stationed at Redstone Arsenal.

Unfortunately, at Huntsville Hospital there were no openings in Delivery room, but now, the nursery—there I could work the day shift! I took the job after the Director of Nurses promised I would get the first opening in the Delivery room. I didn't want to take care of crying babies all day, then go home to four of my own. She seemed to understand, and we had an agreement.

Six weeks after taking the job in the newborn nursery, I was on duty one morning, and was called to the delivery room to receive a newborn baby. There was a new scrub nurse assisting in the delivery. Very casually, I asked her, "Are you new, here, or have you been on a different shift?"

She answered brightly, "Oh, I'm new, but I've had a years' experience." I took the newborn from her, took it to the nursery and started to bathe the infant. My mind was not on my job. A new hire with one year of experience. I'd had seven or eight years of experience, had taken the nursery job in good faith that it would be short term. At my lunch break I took a sheet of paper with me to the cafeteria, and while I ate, I wrote out my resignation, giving the required two weeks' notice. As soon as my shift ended, I went to the Director of Nurses' office and knocked on her door. The Assistant Director answered, and I asked for the Director. "Do you have an appointment?" she asked, nose in the air, not liking to be passed over. "Tell her it is very important that I talk with her," I said. The Director heard me and came out of her office. My temper was up, I was tired, and irritated from listening to babies cry all day. Without preamble, I blurted out, "I met your new Delivery room Nurse this morning." The Director stood there, and I could tell she was recalling our agreement. I wouldn't need to remind her." Oh, yes, we think she will work out very nicely. She is experienced."

"Yes, she told me she'd had a year of experience. I've had seven years,"

"Well, you are doing such a good job in the nursery, everybody is so happy to have you there, we didn't want to make a change there. It's hard to get a good nursery R.N. and you are doing so well –" she ran out of words and stopped. I handed her my resignation, and said, "We had an agreement. I have my own nursery at home. I can't work eight hours every day with crying babies and go home at night to my own." For a moment I felt sorry for the woman—being a Director of Nurses was not an easy job. But she had not kept her word. For a couple of days, if she had come to me, apologized, or offered the next delivery room opening, I might have stayed, but she didn't try to make amends. There was another hospital in town. I worked out my notice and left.

Huntsville was all about Space and it still required both of us working full time, but I found time to go back to school at the branch of University of Alabama, this time to study creative writing, English Literature, History, –all the classes not covered while in Nursing school. Back to work, again as a supervisor, this time on night duty so I could sleep while the kids were in school.

It was my good fortune to have an excellent creative writing instructor, and I took to the class like I'd come home. While a student there, I had my first short story published in the college magazine called, "The Scribbler." That story is reprinted here.

CAVE-IN

Old Jackson hosed down the driveway and the sidewalks near the emergency room every hour in a vain attempt at keeping the black mud out of the halls of the hospital. His kinky silver-haired head moved from side to side with each swing of the mop and he always sang in a soft, monotone negro voice:

> *"When a woman gets the blues, she hangs her head*
> *and cries, when a woman gets the blues, she hangs*

her head and cries, when a man gets the blues, he takes a train and rides, rides, and rides."

Off and on throughout the day Margie would scream at him to stop that infernal moaning, but old Jackson soon would forget and begin again, knowing she was too busy to notice him for long. These last few days Margie had been extremely touchy with her fellow workers, and sometimes short with the patients. She would storm out in unreasonable bursts of temper, fling her red hair over her shoulder, swing her hips and stamp about the emergency room. The only time she seemed approachable was after she removed her white nurses cap and swung the navy- blue cape around her shoulders, ready to go off duty. Then-with responsibility lifted—her smile became friendly and she was almost pretty.

Jackson took his orderly duties seriously. Now the old negro speculated upon the number of young nurses he had seen come and go during his thirty years of service.

"Been a few," he muttered aloud, "been a few."

"What did you say, Jackson?"

"Not a thing, Miss Margie, Not a thing." He picked up his mop and swung it in wide arcs, leaning stiffly from the waist, permanently bent forward, as though his feet couldn't get him there as fast as his head wanted to go.

Johnny sat with his back against the cold black wall. His belt buckle pushed into his abdomen; he brought his knees up to his chest, pushed hard through the dirt-crusted blue denim jacket and gray long-johns underneath. His stubby fingers tugged the belt into a more comfortable position, caressed the smooth silver surface of the buckle, traced the faintly engraved design of a stagecoach. He knew the words, "Wells Fargo" were written on the stagecoach door, could see them even though it was pitch black in the mine. His eyes, rimmed with black coal dust, rolled about, searching for a line of sight, his breathing loud to his ears, loud, ragged, scared, whistling through his nose. Chest tight. Throat pulled in. Afraid to move his tongue. Swallow.

Swallow without spit. He tried again, surprised at the pain caused by the constriction. He concentrated on getting the spit together, but the dust had not yet settled and he choked, coughed aloud. The sound of the cough seemed to circle around, to echo, returning to him, and somehow, he knew it had not traveled far. A hand grabbed his jacket, tightened, warning him to be quiet. Black dirt trickled from the ceiling, slowly, quietly, then –nothing. Black. Cold. Still.

In the Appalachian Mountains January lasts forever. February is more of the same, marked on the calendar, noted by comments heard on street corners:

"Little warmer, today."

"Yup."

"Not long 'til spring now."

"Nope."

"Coal's runnin' low –guess another ton will do?"

"Almanac says it'll thaw early."

"Going to take a little run down to the Capitol if they ever scrape the roads today. You want to go?"

"Might as well, seeing as how you're going anyway."

March: more snow, more high wind, zero readings on the thermometer. The hospital is filled with minor accidents, surgery, routine treatments, and a persistent virus-type influenza. Keep a few beds. . . keep a few beds. . . whispered from supervisor to supervisor . . . for suddenly it is spring, and many are the signs. The thaw begins swiftly, the mountains of snow and ice begin to disappear from the steep slopes and as the snow melts the huge boulders in the river beds are covered with black icy water; the deep banks shrink as the water rises. The highway cinder trucks are washed down to remove the salt and loaded with gravel to fill the chugholes left by the freeze. The heavy winter shutters are removed from the store windows and at the corner service station TIRE CHAINS FOR SALE signs are replaced with FREE CAR WASH WITH FULL TANK OF GAS.

Johnny searched for the car tracks, the small steel rails running into the mine, and when he found them, they felt like strips of ice under his bare hand. He shivered and crouched lower, tightening his leg muscles, drawing double around the belt buckle, feeling it bury into his gut. The hard hat pressed down on the back of his neck, the broken lamp dangled uselessly from the front, ruined with the first rock fall. Water dripped from his nose and fell on the back of his hand and the drop stood, a small bubble rolled in dust. Unconsciously he sniffed and the sound startled him. Again, the hand on his arm tightened.

"Easy, Boy. Don't move."

Ike had twenty-eight years inside, the last ten years on the cutting machine. He ran that monster up the face of the coal, down, back, up, pushing levers and pulling the machine around, up, down, back, cutting, grinding, the bit throwing the dust to the side, black, soft, incessant, unrelenting dust, up, down, back, block after block, hour after hour, year after year, the man as mechanical as the machine, bearing the sharp metal against the black surface, mark, cut, back, crack of solid rock against the steel blade like the crack of hardwood trees in the forest above, high in the mountains when the wind moves and creates distress and branches weep low, touching the rotten foliage, imprinting the snow-covered frozen earth: the crack of tree, the crack of rock, the crack of earth, the slide as water breaks through, melted snow, heavy, black earth with barren branches, matted leaves, pine burrs, empty acorns, the mountain moves and covers the hole. Rocks shift. Earth settles. Now, no sound. Ike whispers, "Don't move."

James Henry Snyder was eleven years old this day. Ma said there would be no sugar for a birthday cake, so he decided to give himself a birthday present – a whole day out of school. That would be his gift to himself, he had done it before, with much less reason. If only Josh would marry his ma, then maybe there would be money for sugar, but Josh said he warn't the marrying kind and Ma didn't ker to push him. Josh worked inside every day and James Henry knew he had money: the mines had been runnin' seven days a week all winter.

James Henry climbed into the big oak tree at the back of the company store and sat straddle the limb. When MacGruder came out the back door to get firewood out of the shed, he'd have plenty of time to snuck in and get an apple. He'd done that before, too. It was a pretty good settin' place, day or night, and he'd used it more than once since Johnny had been running after Suzann MacGruder. Johnny had been over to the MacGruder's most every night since Easter. He knew it was Easter because that was the day the mines didn't run and Josh had bought his Ma a ham for a present, and Suzann had given Johnny that silver belt buckle and told around that they were steadies, her and Johnny. MacGruder must have let that fire go out by now and it warn't that warm. He pulled the hand-me-down sweater closer to his thin body; he'd forgotten how the wind was keener up high.

MacGruder stood at the wooden counter and toted up figures for his customer on a brown paper sack. Arithmetic was hard for him but he had simplified the adding by rounding off the figures, so that .89 cent eggs were now a dollar, and .39 cent bread was fifty cents and you had your choice of the candy for a dime, don't look at the price, just look at the candy, he was fond of saying. With a daughter to raise, now that her mother had run off, he could use the extra. Come spring, he told Susann, come spring you are going to Arizona to your Aunt Sadie. Spring – he turned his head toward the big glass window with its rusted mesh screen and his customer turned with him. A look passed between them and they knew what the other was thinking.

"Thawed too fast," said MacGruder.

"Yep," replied the miner. "They's drilling today too."

MacGruder knew. Ike had said last night that he was running the monster today. Ike said, too, that he was gettin' out this spring. Said last night he'd go with him and Susann to Arizona, said he thought it'd be good for his black lung. MacGruder and Ike. More than twenty years together, most of it inside. He raised his head again and listened closely, suddenly wary and afraid of some undetermined quality . . . was that a sound? No, more just a feeling . . . .

Margie checked the supply cabinet again, nervous, jittery, plasma, dressings, splints, she worried about the readiness of her emergency trays, checked the dates on suture sets. Her new job did not seem to be what she had expected. The newspaper ad had seemed so beautiful: Day shift—which she would never get in her own training hospital as a new graduate—room and board, salary open. It was the ideal place to gain experience since she was considered the Head Nurse in her unit. But shortly after her arrival she had noted the worried looks on the women's faces, watched the miner's concern over the weather conditions as the temperature began to rise. In some areas the roads were completely gone, washed away, necessitating detours of several miles. She heard the dreaded words, 'cave-in' from every direction and listened covertly to descriptions of mining accidents. She tried to recall her classes in disaster nursing and ruefully admitted that she had not listened at all.

"Jackson!"

"Yes, Miss Margie?"

"Please hush!"

"Yes, ma'am, Miss Margie."

The old negro spread a clean sheet on the carrier by the emergency room door and professionally squared the corners. He avoided looking directly at the young nurse and chuckled as she walked away. "*Don't worry, Miss Margie,*" he said softly, "*When that whistle blow, you'll have plenty of help.*"

"*What did you say, Jackson?*" called Margie over her shoulder.

"*Nothin', Miss Margie, nothin'.*"

Johnny took the hard hat from his head and rubbed the dark matted hair; he jerked the broken lamp off the hat and used it to scrape the mud off his miner's boots. He eased his legs out from under him slowly, first one, then the other. Was he right? Was the water beginning to rise? He stretched his legs several times, then crouched on his heels again. He felt around and before him, trying to reach Ike, missing Ike's hand now that it no longer gripped his arm.

"*Ike?*" Softly.

Thin panic slipped into his voice. Again, stronger, "*Ike?*"

"*Yeah, it's all stopped. You can talk now. It won't move again.*"

"*Where's Josh?*"

"*He got out I think.*"

Johnny moved slowly, pain beginning in the calves of his legs, back scrubbing the black wall of coal. Ike stopped him.

"*Where you goin'?*"

"*See how bad.*"

"*Sit still. I've done that. Can't hear nobody call if you move around.*"

"*Ike? Ike! You got no light either?*"

"*No, no light, Johnny. So why don't you just take a nap?*'

"*Ike?*"

"*Thought Josh was up ahead.*"

"*Go to sleep, Johnny. He'll send them after us.*"

Johnny fingered the silver buckle and thought about Suzann, how pleased she had been to give it to him. "*It's a real Western Buckle, Johnny, from Arizona. Uncle sent it to Pa, but he only wears bibs.*" He had just started to kiss her when that danged James Henry showed up, damn kid, sneaking around, too skinny to beat up. He'd give him a nickel to get lost the next time he spotted him up in that tree.

Susann sat cross-legged in the orange rocker on her front porch. It was fairly warm in the sun, as long as she was out of the wind. The blue jeans and protruding pink sweater front were sprinkled with cracker crumbs as she alternated between a bite of cracker, a bite of cooking cheese. Johnny would be coming out of the mine soon and she didn't plan to miss him. She drummed her fingers on the wooden porch railing and stopped to sip MOUNAIN DEW from the green bottle sitting on the unpainted floor. She smiled secretly, playing her favorite game, "What shall I give him tonight?" She had nearly run out of things, first the pink hair ribbon, then her charm bracelet from the five and dime, then, best of all, Pa's silver buckle. Lately, all she'd had to give him was herself, a kiss, a hug, and last night, when he unbuttoned the top of her blouse, just to look, he said, breath sucked in, smile widened, eyes bright as she relived the excitement of anticipation. She wouldn't go too far like Maybelle Tucker had done and get into trouble, just far enough to get him to marry her. He had a job now, and inside was good money even if he did come out so black, and they could live right here with Pa, she wouldn't go to Arizona. They'd sleep in her bed—she shivered at the thought. She brushed the crumbs from her sweater, softly touching her breast and smiled again.

She rubbed the nipple lightly with her finger, glad it stood out straight, showing through the sweater, instead of drooping down like James Henry's Ma —what did Josh see in her? She was older than him. Once Suzann thought Josh was going to come calling on her, but Pa said he was too old, and it didn't matter no how, now that Johnny was coming. What would it be like to be kissed by a man as old as Josh? But he seemed to be a regular over at James Henry's house these days —James Henry! If she caught him spying on her again, she'd hit him with a rock! She touched her breast again *and smiled. She knew what she could give him tonight and come spring....*

Margie counted the narcotics carefully, checking each tablet and ampule, signing her name on each page of the book. Safe again. Off duty.

"It hasn't rained today, Jackson. The danger is past when the rain stops, isn't it?"

"No, ma'am, Miss Margie. It ain't that way."

"But if the rain stops the floods go down, right?"

"No, Miss Margie. Not if they's still snow on the mountains."

James Henry eased further up in the tree, stretched across the bare limb and wished for leaves. Hope he don't look up. He could see right down into MacGruder's backyard. Come warm weather Johnny is going to have that Suzann right on the grass below him. He got into her shirt last night, won't be long. If'n he takes his pants off I'll get that silver buckle without him ever knowing it, but he'll probably do it with his pants on like Josh does when he comes to see Ma. Won't have a chance lessen he takes them off. Wonder what's keeping MacGruder, he's let that fire go out by now fer sure.

MacGruder had the column of figures half added when the whistle blew. He laid down the stub of a pencil, untied the flour-sack apron and started for the mine, his customer right behind him. MacGruder had heard that whistle before, the last time when that jackleg operation over the hill had caved in and damn near killed him when he tried to help get the men out. He remembered the sound as he ran for the mine, same as now, the wail unlike any other on earth, the wild, desperate grind of the hand-turned siren; he knew the feel of the steel crank as the ear-splitting noise began to be blocked out by the fear lying cold inside you, cold with the certain knowledge that the top had give: MacGruder had worked inside before coming to the company store.

Suzann's long legs in their blue jeans hit the floor running, running, running, breath coming hard and fast, silently no, no,

God, no, forgetting to put down the cheese, carrying it in her hand, cracker crumbs on her chin, faintly, running, running, and only salt left when she reached the motor barn.

James Henry slid down the tree on his belly and took a short cut through MacGruder's backyard, across the school lot forgetting he was supposed to be in class, under the rail fence through old Ike's garden plot where there warn't any crops but old Ike still shouted get out of my garden, up the hill to the tracks, past the tipple and the wash shed to the car shop—the car shop, where they'd be counting the head lamps to see who didn't come out —hearing the horn the whole time and thinking maybe he'd be in time to turn it some hisself.

Margie placed her cap inside the white cabinet and reached for her cape. The sound startled her, low, moving slowly, then louder, faster, louder, louder until it filled the room crowding into the corners louder into her head her head her head would burst, burst burst! No! She was off duty now. She didn't have to stay. She didn't know what to do first Jackson—Jackson—she began to run back to the emergency room, "Jackson!"

"Here's your call list, Miss Margie, right here on the back of this door, now, while you make your calls, I'll l jest be getting' ready."

Yes, of course. The first step. Notify key personnel. She dialed the first number, forgetting that the whole town could hear the whistle too.

"Ike?"

"Be still, Boy. Save yer air. We'll hear them coming if you'll be still."

Johnny explored the wall with his fingers, but any movement stirred up the bug dust and made it harder to breathe. The rocks were still now. The machine was totally buried. He circled the small area in a few short moves, almost without changing his crouched position. He coughed lightly and felt the dust between his teeth, gritty and tasteless, dry. He had to get some relief for his legs, straightened them out to sit, but he would be sitting in water, and the ceiling was less than thirty inches high. He took off his silver belt buckle, grasped the buckle in his palm, wrapped the leather belt around and around his hand, it won't get lost, Suzann, then he lay down in the water,

"Ike?"

"Be still, Boy, they'll come."

The miner's lamps hung in rows in the car shop with spaces for the ones still inside. One by one the men came out ad hung their lamp in its accustomed place, the surest way to know who was inside and who had come out. There were nine lamps missing. Rescue operations began,

"Pa! Pa! Where's Johnny?"

"Go home, Suzann! Go home! You will just be in the way!"

"Mr. MacGruder, is Josh – ""

"Git home, Kid! Git back up in yore tree!"

"MacGruder! MacGruder! Pump house! Hurry! The pump is jammed!"

By dark the cutting through was finished, and within four hours the bones were set, sutures in, bandages applied. Beds were found and the families sent home.

Now the six men lay in the big ward, silent, smoking or chewing Brown Mule and spitting into emesis basins. Now they talked, softly, one at a time, with long silences between their comments.

"Not as bad as the one back in '67."

"Wished I'd had a watch, kept wanting to know what time it was."

"Lost my dinner first thing ---hadn't et neither."

"Used to work with a fellow, said he would eat his dinner first thing as soon as he got inside, didn't want the rats to get it."

"Josh always said that's the way he'd go."

"Yeh," Quietness, and smoke drifting upward.

"Ike was the best there was on that damned machine."

"Somebody said the kid had taken off his belt and was holding the buckle in his hand,"

Then a young man hoisted himself up to one elbow and, grinning, said," Know what I thought about most?"

"What?"

"Wondered who'd take my wife to my funeral! Haw! Haw!"

An older, grizzled man answered in a soft voice, "Shet yore damn mouth!"

Margie didn't realize her cap was not on until she opened the cabinet door to put it away. She ran her hands through her red hair; her legs trembled and her back ached from the long hours on her feet. Nothing is as bad as it seems. The tough part is the dreading it. A few more months of this and I can apply in the city. Jackson moved his mop bucket out of the way as she walked to the door.

"It wasn't as bad as I thought it would be, Jackson," she said.

He leaned on his mop handle and watched her go. For a brief moment she was a white silhouette against the dark mountain rising above the town, then she grew smaller and smaller, disappeared. Jackson picked up his mop and slowly, methodically, wiped her footprints away.

After several years as Night Supervisor, the opportunity to transfer to Industrial Nursing presented itself, with an increase in pay and an opportunity to study while at work.

I pursued a degree with English as a major, something I had longed for all the years I had worked as a nurse, a dream job, work five days a week with every weekend off, and out of school all summer when the children were home. A desk job with no more running up three flights of stairs when the elevator wasn't fast enough, juggling staff, struggling to cover last-minute absences by doing double duty, Oh, that would be a dream! A teacher! An English teacher!

Once, in my second year of nurses training, I just couldn't take it any longer. I had quit. I quit and went home. No more emergencies, surgeries in the middle of the night —once at two a.m. during an appendectomy on a ten year old boy, I fainted, knocked over my instrument tray as I fell, made the surgeon wait while the circulating nurse brought a new tray, ruined his record for doing an appendectomy in less than ten minutes. I woke up on a carrier in the hall, parked beside an open window, where the night breeze moved. No air-conditioning in those days. That surgeon never spoke to me again, but I learned by the grapevine that he still requested me as scrub nurse.

The Industrial Nurse "position" (it was not a job) was all I expected.

Nearly the only woman in the plant on the night shift, I was treated like a queen. All I had to do was ask, and if it was possible, it was done. The emergencies were child's play compared to what I had handled in the emergency room, and after correctly diagnosing kidney stones, when the man was sure he was having a heart attack, my word was never questioned. The insurance record keeping was a major part of the work requirement, but that was a sit-down job and no worse than all the endless charting in the hospital. And I could attend classes in the day hours, while the kids were in school, be home when they got home, get supper, go to football games, take them to scouts, cheer-leading, gymnastics, children's choir, Sunday school, church, and endless birthday parties, a full-time chauffer. And the new job provided new material for short stories!

FRANK

It started innocently. It was early fall, when the leaves were changing, and he seemed so simple, uncomplicated, seemingly as open as his appearance, coming in quiet and easy-like, unassuming, his slight frame taking leisurely paced steps around her desk to the blue box on the counter.

"All dressed up this morning, ain't ya," he said, "like you was somebody."

She looked up, laughed self-consciously, glancing down at her blue suit skirt and high-heeled shoes.

"Just a change," she said, "I get so tired of white, white all the time, all the time—" She stopped short, aware she was running on inordinately long, conscious of his long, light eyelashes as he looked at her. They curl, she marveled. His eyelashes curled.

"Where's your Tylenol? I can't take aspirin."

She moved to the blue box, searched among the packets and extracted one. He smiled gently and strolled toward the door.

"Wait! I don't know your name!"

She bumped the blue box, it toppled, and she grabbed for it awkwardly. He was beside her, righting the box, replacing it on the counter. "For my log," she said quickly, "for my records."

"Frank," he said, sweet, lazy smile, movement of one hand toward the name printed in white letters on his industrial-blue shirt. "See ya."

Irritated, she organized the contents of the pill box, straightened her navy skirt and white lab coat, resumed her chair at the desk.

He was back the next morning, coming in just before seven, smiling gently, helping himself to the Tylenol in the black and white industrial packets: he'd known all along. This time she knocked her Job-Injury notebook off her desk. He retrieved it, calm, gentle, watching her confusion with something like kindness.

By the end of the week he was bringing her coffee from the Canteen machine, setting it on her desk, light smile, brown curls loose and tousled, almost childishly uncombed. The next week he sat briefly in her treatment chair, looked at the morning paper, reading only the comic strips while she worked, companionable in his silence. Another employee came in, hobbling on a sprained ankle, and Frank stepped in, "Here, you'll get dirty from his boot," helped the man remove his hard-toed shoe, tilted back the chair to elevate the foot. Frank took the instant ice packs, crushed them easily between his hands to activate them. With a wave, he was gone, leaving her to place the ice bags around the injured ankle.

Days went by, and each morning she waited for him to appear, building long conversations with him in her mind, things to share with him, to ask him —was he married? But she knew, no need to ask she had his record in her file. How long had he worked at the plant? Inwardly she saw his smile, imagined him saying, simply, quietly, "You know. You've looked it up," and thought, too, how embarrassed she'd be if he confronted her with it.

Gradually the sense of waiting began to build. He was there to fill the cup dispenser when she couldn't reach it, stretching upward smoothly, gracefully. Another time, and the patient had a back strain, was giving her vague, conflicting details of an accident to explain his injury. Frank, standing at the water cooler, his back against the wall, slow, mocking smile, explained, "He wants a week off work." The man sputtered, red-faced, objecting, and Frank spoke softly, "Deer season opens tomorrow."

She sent the man back to work over his loud objections, and five minutes later the phone rang, his supervisor, laughing, full of praise as he commended her for her decision. "It was a set-up", he explained, "they were making bets in the locker room that he'd get out of work! How did you know?"

"Nursing judgement," she said, seeing Frank's smile as he'd said, 'deer season'. She owed him one.

Late fall, and fresh pears appeared on her desk, Thanksgiving, and a bag of pecans. A large man came into the clinic early one morning, blood dripping from one hand, straining to get to the stainless-steel sink. Frank, sitting in the treatment chair, paper in his hands, saw him first and moved the chair, his chair, behind the huge man just as he fainted and fell.

Calm again, the patient on his way to the doctor, she looked around. Frank had quietly gone back to work. Without him, she reflected, the large man would have hit the floor. The incidents collected, became commonplace, expected.

Christmas and the two-week plant shut down was approaching. The accident rate rose daily as the men, long accustomed to beating the system, tried to arrange an injury that would keep them off work and on Workman's Compensation over the holidays, thus drawing double pay, a 'Christmas bonus' of sorts. A back strain, or twisted knee, a hurt shoulder, or elbow—every minor ache and pain was magnified into a serious injury, and she struggled to hold the line, to keep them working. Two weeks to go, ice packs, heat packs, pills and salves, anything except sending them home with medical certification.

One week to go, elbow straps, wrist bands, knee braces, patch 'em up, return 'em to work, keep the machines running, the tires rolling off the conveyor's, filling the eighteen-wheelers and the railroad cars, filling the year-end quotas, running extra shifts, pushing, straining toward the two-week break.

Only three days to go. Frank did not come in. All day she looked for him, expecting him each time the door opened. The day was long, and she was uneasy, restless, disorganized.

Two days to go. Frank did not come. She couldn't ask about him, what reason would she give? All morning she watched and waited. After lunch she decided to walk through the plant, vaguely admitting to herself that she had to know.

She walked down the hall from the clinic, past the offices, and opened the double doors into the production area. The noise hit her like a wall, machinery whining, forklifts rumbling, tuggers clanging as they pulled high-loaded A-frames. The sharp, pungent odor of carbon and rubber filled her nostrils, taking her breath. The dirt and disorder were noticeable.

She walked carefully between the tire-building machines, one eye on the moving vehicles, the other watching for Frank. She saw him almost immediately, and he saw her.

She paused beside him, watched as he folded and slit hot rubber, cutting it on an angle, spinning the green-carcass drum. He didn't look up, never acknowledged her presence, slitting and cutting the black rubber, hot knife flashing on the bias, returned to its hot cup, more sheets of thin black rubber pulled down, slashed, drum spinning, the rhythm of his movements graceful, smooth, mesmerizing. She turned, confused, and retreated.

As she opened the clinic door the quiet, after the machinery, was tangible. She looked about, clean white counters, fresh disinfectant odor, the orderliness and preciseness of shining stainless steel containers. The peacefulness struck her as never before. She sat at her desk, studying her small area, her one-room domain, feeling lonely yet calm and detached. She had felt lost in the plant, but here, here she was in command. This was her territory.

The door opened, and Frank stood before her, unsmiling, quiet and still. "Make me out a report. I've hurt my back."

"Oh—Frank! How!"

"Never mind how, just do it!

"But--?" She reached toward him, but he stepped back, avoiding her touch. His smile returned, cold, reserved, and he held her eyes with his own. Slowly she grasped his intention: He had been planning this all along!

Not taking her eyes from his, she found her desk chair, eased herself into it and leaned back. "Take two aspirin and call me in the morning," she said, raising her chin.

Frank's face relaxed. His old smile came sliding back, widened into a grin.

"Now," he said, "now you're somebody!"

He waved at her gently. "See ya."

—⚬—

HAPPINESS

I sat alone in a darkened room
And watched the laden sky.
I saw the cars pass on the road
And heard the pine trees sigh.

The children played not far away
And left me quietness.
A single girl would never know
This happiness.

The wind picks up
And clouds press down.
The children cease their game—
And with the rain, Daddy came.

His look of love embraced his own
And moved the darkness by.
Deep content, a day well-spent,
Was wrapped within my sigh.

~Betty Roberts

My husband got an opportunity to go to the Kwajalein Islands as an instructor for the Army. He was now teaching the Niki Hercules missile system and would earn a bonus for the two-year tour.

We all had our passport photos made, planned what to take and he went for his physical, one of the last requirements. During the exam, the Doctor picked up hypertension. He put it down to anxiety, told him to come back in a week, which he did. His blood pressure was still dangerously elevated. His transfer was cancelled. We were very disappointed.

During these years, my husband had been taking classes at the University of Alabama in Huntsville, with a master's degree as his goal. He had accumulated the first twelve hours, but the remainder of credits necessary for a master's had to be taken on the Tuscaloosa campus. We had bought our first house, a new three bedroom, located only a few miles from the Arsenal where he taught. I loved our lives, happy with my job, the kids able to walk to the elementary school, a good church, close friends, but his plans for furthering his education took precedence over all of this. We could buy another house, the kids would always have a good school, I could get a job anywhere. We sold the house, took the profit and moved to Tuscaloosa. He was right: I could get a job anywhere –provided I just took whatever was available. Never, in all of my years in Nursing, never had I dreamed of working in a State-owned Mental institution. My choices for a job in Tuscaloosa were, night duty in the University Hospital, a drive of some distance, or day shift at the mental institution, which was very near the College Campus. On the up side, I would make more money at the mental institution, would be Day Supervisor in the Men's Receiving Building, every other weekend off, and on the weekends when I was on duty, I would make rounds in all of the other buildings. Of course, that was my choice, and at last, I was off night duty.

The only fly in our cream was my husband's health. In spite of medication, his blood pressure continued to be abnormally high and of major concern.

We settled into college life again like we were born to it: classes, walking across beautiful grounds well-kept with fall foliage turning rainbow colors, football games, with student tickets. Our four children wore matching red sweaters, Alabama colors, and made their spending money by parking cars on our lawn for the games. They walked to school, we went to the closest church, and the year passed swiftly.

Never let it be said that I didn't take advantage of an opportunity. While my husband completed a Master's in Education, I took creative writing classes from some of the best instructors ever, and with weekends off, was able to attend workshops I never would have been able to attend in Huntsville.

MATTRESS MAN

As the metal door shut behind him, Mr. St. John protested: "I don't see why you have to take all of my clothes. I've told you; I can't help you. Can't do a thing about your pool table."

He stood before the desk and emptied his pockets, his movements slow and studied. He concentrated, frowning as he removed keys, cigarettes, lighter, billfold, some loose change, and a small metal case. The case was two inches square, thin silver on one side, beautifully engraved, grey Mother-of Pearl on the other side, an antique, clearly valuable. Inside it contained a thin measuring tape, the numbers worn off for the first two inches from years of constant use.

His hands were shaking as he unbuttoned his washed-out shirt, hung it on the back of a straight chair, and stood naked to the waist. He was tall, thin, slightly stooped, and the few hairs on his chest were white. His face was thin, red-flushed, not brown but he

79

seemed to belong in the sun for he smelled of fresh grass and the heat of the fields —he would look more at home on the seat of a tractor, bent over the wheel, his light-colored eyes following the blade of a mower or the furrow of the plow. Yet, his hands were soft and white with round-trimmed nails, cleaner than most, like the hands of a shopkeeper or clerk.

"I measure mattresses," he said, "have for years. My company doesn't handle anything but mattresses and sofa pillows—we do a lot of sofa pillows—but we never do pool tables. Not now. Charlie used to send me to measure the pool tables, but he said I couldn't get back same day, so he quit doing them. Here's what I do: I answer the phone and some little old lady tells me she has an antique bed or maybe it's an antique cradle, or a French sofa —so I go out, measure it and give an estimate on the cost of covering it, then Charlie does all the work. Charlie says I'm the best at giving estimates, never let him lose any money. Use to help with the work, but now . . ..

Charlie says we can't come out on pool tables, but I tell him, we charge a little more, people who play pool got money, they can pay more."

A nurse quietly gathered up the personal belongings, placed his admission papers on a clip board and left the room. A young man, muscular, blonde and shaven, dressed in white short-sleeved uniform of an attendant, continued with tagging the old man's clothing and ignored his insistent explanations. Mr. St. John took the white muslin pajamas from the chair and slowly put them on, his knees bending awkwardly as he swayed, nearly losing his balance, shifting from one foot to the other. The attendant led him into the next room and settled him in another straight-backed chair.

The Day room was impressively large with plain white walls, red concrete floor and naked windows curtained only with a steel mesh screen. There were two heavy wooden tables, each large enough to seat twelve men, some chairs, a green water cooler that was adjusted to run continuously, and three metal spittoons, one at each end of the room and one by the water cooler. Several men, each dressed in unmatched pants and shirts, were sitting about the room, playing cards, talking, or just staring; each seemed alone in his own way. A door opened at the far end of the room and an attendant shouted, "Let's eat!"

The men lined up, single file, silently taking their places as though assigned their positions at some previous time, and slowly moved out of the room. Mr. St. John rose to follow but a firm hand on his shoulder stopped him. "Please, sit down. When your clothes have been marked you will be allowed to go to the dining room with the others, but, for today, I'll bring your lunch to you."

Mr. St. John had been unaware of the presence of the nurse and he briefly considered her. "I don't want lunch. I didn't come here to eat. I came to measure your mattresses. Charlie said you had a big order, a lot of work, and he was giving me one more chance. I'm sorry about your pool table, but we don't do that anymore."

"Please, Mr. St. John, sit down. We will bring your lunch right here."

It seemed strange that she placed the tin tray on the pool table, but he diffidently picked up the spoon. He saw yellow sunflowers with dark round seeds on the tray and when he touched it with his spoon the seeds began to move up the handle and onto his hand. In desperation, he threw the spoon and swung his fist to shake them off. The seeds grew to giant proportions and changed from black to white. They held his arms and tightened across his shoulders, half-carried, half-pulled him away from the pool table and down a long corridor with white walls and the floor was red and wavy, like a moving sea of wine and the light at the end stung his eyes in its brightness, exploded as he was released abruptly. He fell forward on his face and landed on a mattress.

At last. This was familiar. He welcomed the blue and white stripped ticking. This was why he had come. He hunted for his tape measure. Length, width, thickness —but the tape was gone. Perhaps he had left it in his coat pocket. He stood unsteadily and tried the door, but there was no door handle. His fingers explored the smooth metal plate and found the keyhole, passed upwards, over the edge of a narrow grill above, then down to the floor. A drink would help. He hadn't had one for several hours now, and he was shaking. Always before, when he started to sweat, a short one helped. He reached for the bottle sitting before him on the floor, but just as he nearly touched it, he heard someone calling his name. "Mr. St. John! Mr. St. John!"

"Lily," he said. "And she's mad again. Always says "Mr." when she is all out done. I'd know that crabby voice anywhere...leave that bottle alone, Mr.! ...after twenty-two years wouldn't you think she'd know I'm going to suit myself? She sure knows how to get under a man's skin. Shut up, Lily!"

He put his hand out to get the bottle, but now it was sitting just outside the door. He could see it through the wooden slats, but the spaces were too narrow for his hand to go through. "Funny door. Holes in it. No, not holes. Stripes. Red and white stripes. Red. White, red, white, wine and champagne, roses and lilies, Lilies. Damn you, Lily! Bring me a drink!"

"Bugs again! No, not bugs, snakes! Pa! Git the hoe, Pa!

"Humph, what's the matter with me. Pa's been gone a long time."

"Who? Who's calling me? I'll be right there, soon as I measure this mattress. Thirty-six inches, Charlie, now, how long? "

"Sure Charlie, sure. I'm ready to eat, what did ya bring today—more of that God-awful pepperoni?"

He took the tray being offered and sat down on the floor, but when he touched it the food began changing places, moving, crawling, crossing the metal partitions. Perspiration stood out on his face and the spoon rattled against the metal tray. In one convulsive movement he shoved the tray across the room and jumped up, braced the wall, his arms spread stiff against its surface, bare feet clawing for a grip on the red concrete. He began to shout for help. "Someone come here! Anyone! Help me hold this damn wall! Help me!" For a long time, he sweated and strained, pushed, pleaded, until at last he slipped down onto the mattress, exhausted.

He lay face down until some of the trembling went away and then a movement beyond the door caught his attention. He rolled over twice and lay against the door, his right cheek pressed against the concrete and his right eye to the crack under the door. He could see across the hall to another wall, rising white and cold, like a mist rising above the red river of concrete, rising gently, the cold fear in his throat, the deep, cold fear like mist over the river, white, moving, rising. . . .

"Jack! Hey, Jack! Where are you, man? Damn it, Jack!"

The white mist crept just above the water line, an illusion of wall, firm, tangible; he reached out to touch it and felt the emptiness. A bull frog throbbed once, deep voiced, echoed in the fog and was silent, lost in the hushed sound of swift black water. Jack had been right here beside him as they stole through the night, shuttered lantern, tin bucket, searching for the trot line, ready with fresh bait. The bank, red, wet clay, moving beneath their feet, crumbling …he caught a small branch as the bank slid into the water. "Jack! Get my hand! Jack! Jack!"

He fell sobbing to the ground, shivering, his best friend gone in the dark water, a sinkhole, unknown, the cold, swift water undercutting the bank. White mist moved before his eyes, separated into thin wisps, drifting slowly. He shook, thin hands pressed down tightly….

Thin hands pressed down, veins standing out with the pressure against the cold red floor, the red concrete floor. The white walls moved in, surrounded him, and softly he whispered, "Jack, Jack. Jack." He closed his eyes and slept.

But the reprieve was brief. In less than two hours, he was awake. The sound of a machine reached him, a steady hum that he had trouble identifying. Then he knew. "Pa! Git that boy away from that tractor!"

The last time the boy had started the tractor ... he jumped to his feet and rushed to the door. He could hear the machine, close, just out of sight. He grew dizzy with the image of his son riding the high seat in his cut-off jeans and cowboy hat, young shoulders freckled from the sun, skin taut and firm with budding muscles and excessive energy, riding high, fancy boots clamped on the clutch throwing it out of gear, the tractor running wild and rough down the meadow toward the ditch a few feet away –the ditch hidden in stickweed, milkweed and multiflora roses with thorns making a thicket, running, running, coarse and dangerous. . ..

"Lily! Lily! Git the boy! Oh, God! He'll be killed! Lily, Git the boy, git the boy!"

He shook the door, tears streaming down his face, groping for a handle, trembling with fear. He tried to see through the narrow slats, but he couldn't see the tractor and the boy wouldn't be able to hear above the noise. The boy didn't know about the ditch, hadn't tried to mow along the edge of the gully like he had, hadn't sweated out one bad slip in wet grass and slick clay, before the weeds covered it, before the briars and thorny roses ...at last the noise stopped.

"Lily, it warn't my fault, I didn't see him coming, didn't know he was anywhere about ...damn it, Lily! Don't take on so! I miss him too ...I miss him too..."

The old man looked about with a pathetic expression when a hand gripped his shoulder with compassion. He didn't know this young stranger in the white suit, but it didn't matter. His nerves were gone. He couldn't take anymore. A drink would steady him. He was shaking, cold, no—hot. "Listen, Charlie, I'll give you twenty dollars for one good drink of whiskey."

He fumbled in his pajama pocket and then looked around the room. "I've got it. You ask Lily. She'll tell you—I've always got money. Found it in a mattress! Ask Lily! She'll tell you, says I'm the luckiest mattress man she's ever seen! I won it in a pool game, but I never told her. She don't like me to play poker, says that's when I get the whiskey. She don't know. First comes the whiskey, then comes the pool. Use to play pretty good, never got beat, good money, then she found out; she messes up everything! Says I'm throwing my money away. Hell, I've made more than I've ever lost!"

He was handed a cup of water, and drained the cup, then turned the cup over his toes. "Have to put on my shoes, feet cold." He sat on the mattress and rolled the paper cup against the wall, watched its erratic return. "Why do bottles never roll straight? It comes back but not where it started from!" He rolled the cup again, watched as it rolled into a corner. "People can't go back," he said, "and people don't roll straight neither!"

The nurse tried to place a thermometer under his tongue, but he couldn't keep his mouth closed, could not control his chin. He raised his hand to steady it but the gesture was misunderstood and she grabbed his arm. When she left the room, he decided to find Charlie, tell him he was sorry, but he had made a mess out of this call, hadn't been able to measure a single mattress—maybe Charlie had his tape!

He ran up the hall, the nurse leaving the door open, slipping on the newly waxed and buffed floor, his feet searching for some means of support, his arms flailing wildly, a thin, inarticulate cry forming in his throat. "Charlie! Let it go! Damn it, Charlie, what's wrong with you?"

He sagged to the floor, was caught, then carried, face down, the red floor swimming beneath him, steel steps, then green title. Doors were unlocked, relocked with a steel clang and dull thud of bolt, hands bit into his flesh and strained at the corners of his pajamas until, finally, he was rolled into —hay, loose and soft, sweet-smelling red clover, a hint of a sneeze in his nostrils, a scratchiness on face and elbows.

The hay was hot and dry, and he heard the hum of insects, felt the sting of a bee, and the scratching of a grasshopper in the bend of his elbow. He was on his father's farm and someone was with him, Lily, or his mother, he couldn't be sure, no, it wouldn't be Lily. She had never liked the farm. It was Lily who had kept him in town, Lily who had kept him with Charlie all these years, saying don't trade a sure thing for a fly-by-night deal, every time he had a better offer. All these years, even after Pa died and his Mother needed him on the land.

When he tried to open his eyes, he was swimming in a river and could only see a pale light through waves of water, but he had always gone swimming after the hay was shocked, down through the fresh fields of cut golden stubble, past old rabbits nests and clumps of briar ivy that had escaped the mower, to the stream lined with white-barked sycamores and wine-purple elderberry bushes. The water was cold; he shivered, unable to control himself. He tried to swim faster, to get warm, to reach the bank before the cramps set in but he couldn't use his arms. His hands were tied, and he fought to free them. It was no use. He ceased to struggle.

Now he was floating, gently rising and falling, neither hot nor cold, conscious only of not being alone. Frequently he heard voices, often the voice called his name. It seemed to be the same voice, but he couldn't be sure. Gradually, he noticed other sounds, a soft, mechanical purr near enough to touch, the clang of metal on metal, a plastic crackling of the mattress beneath him, a familiar sound, for he had put hundreds of covers on mattresses and he knew their ways.

He went to sleep and knew he slept; he recognized night from day. He drank from a straw held to his lips and felt the touch of hands: he knew he had been a long time coming to this.

He opened his eyes and saw the oxygen mask, the infusion bottles with their thin plastic tubes and he moved his hands, feeling the bonds that restrained him, strong leather straps buckled to the iron bed railing. He saw the nurse beside the bed and tried to speak but his mouth was dry, and his throat ached.

The nurse removed the oxygen mask and offered a drink of water. "Hello, Mr. St. John," she said, "Welcome back."

He held the cool water in his mouth until it warmed then swallowed carefully. He thought she looked familiar but couldn't place her, watched as she moved about the bed, inspecting the infusion, turning the green oxygen valve to off, straightening the white sheets. Even her voice was familiar. Then, he remembered her.

"Nurse," he said.

"Yes, Mr. St. John?"

He cleared his throat and tried again. "Nurse?"

"Yes?"

"Where did you put my Tape Measure?"

I was back to job hunting again. We had no idea where we would be going, and, determined to stay out of the snow-country, my husband had applications all over the south. Two weeks before his final graduation exercises, we decided to drive up to Huntsville to visit our good friends. They all gathered at one house for a cook-out. In mid-afternoon—it was a Sunday—one of the men called me into a bedroom to talk in private. He asked, how would you like to come back to Huntsville? I burst into tears, and with a big hug, he said, "Let me see what I can do." I rejoined the others around the grill.

About thirty minutes later, this gentleman took my husband around the corner of the house. They were gone several minutes, and when they came back, our friend called for everybody's attention. With his arm around my husband's shoulders, he announced, "Well, folks, you can welcome these friends back to town! They have accepted their old job back!" Needless to say, the children and I were overjoyed.

We began years of checking his blood pressure, giving medications, doctor after doctor, diagnosis, at that time, Malignant Hypertension. Finally, in desperation, we went to Ochsner clinic in New Orleans, he and I, leaving our four kids in the hands of our friends. After endless tests, it was decided the problem stemmed from a congenital deformity of the artery leading to his kidney, and the diagnosis was renamed Renal Artery Hypertension. Surgery was the only treatment.

Five weeks later we came home, his blood pressure fairly normal. Eight months later our fifth child was born prematurely, and the older four took over, becoming her 'mother or father' as needed while I returned to nursing.

Although my husband had returned to work, he struggled with periods of depression which became obvious as he threatened suicide. He took his own life with a twenty-two rifle, in spite of all we could do. The story of his death, and the disastrous effect on the children and I, as well as upon his parents and sisters became my first published book as I turned to my writing as a means of coping with the many emotions and problems involved in becoming a widow at forty.

LEANING INTO THE WIND

The Wilderness of Widowhood
By Betty Bryant
(Excerpt from the book published under pen name)

One of the courses I was taking at the University at this time was Psychology. I was reading with interest about the phenomenon of "transference". This Freudian concept states that a person in therapy transfers to the therapist feelings concerning another individual, rather than seeing the therapist as he is. I read of the matter with amusement, for I had already agreed to weekly talks with my minister; I had actually joked with him about needing the psychiatrist's couch.

I dismissed the theories about transference as absurd, for at this time I was totally caught up in the realization that my husband had willingly left me—had publicly rejected me. I was trying to rationalize his suicide both to myself and others in terms of his illness. The rationalization ran a circular route: he killed himself because he didn't love me. . .but he was ill…and being ill he didn't want to be a burden, so he did love me. . . but if he loved me why did he leave me?

I felt no real need to confide in anyone. Counseling sessions would only provide an opportunity for crying on someone's shoulder—and what was there to cry about?

My minister had brought me home from the emergency room, helped with the family, preached the funeral, and either called or came by daily, ready to catch me when I fell. But isn't that what ministers are for? They marry you, bury you, preach to you on Sunday. Now I had an urgent need not to be preached to, but to be listened to. My minister filled that role also. My next journal entry articulated that need:

Encircled. Surrounded. Surrounded by children, family, friends. Yet the space around me is empty. There is no one person to turn to, no single soul to care. Maybe he didn't talk to me like he used to—is that so important? He listened to me and now there is no one to do that. He was my buffer zone, my insulation from the rest of the world.

As my weekly conferences with the minister continued, I began to realize how often I was seeing him: Wednesday night at choir practice, Sunday morning and Sunday night, my conference hour, and often through the week at his house or mine for his children were friends with my children too. At the next conference he took my hand and told me I was a lovely woman. In that moment, with that one touch, I fell in love. I had no warning of the emotional turmoil that was to follow:

Wanting you is like an ache in every nerve cell, a reaching out from the depths of my being to join you in every way a woman could join a man. Although you will never know how I care, the wild expectations which I entertained for a few moments were precious to me. It is enough just to love. If I could never reach completion in the way you could make me whole, if I must go bound by convention, if I must be the one to love and never be loved in return, then so be it. It is still better than the cold isolation I have felt for the past few weeks; it is better to know that I am, indeed, alive.

I am alone. Betty is gone. Only Mom is left, and Nurse, and friend. I must pull away from you lest you guess my feelings, for when I am near you, I cannot resist the impulse to go to you; I am pulled by an irresistible force; there is no end to the desire to be near you.

Am I ill? Is this the beginning of complete separation? I fear a division of my personality. Isolation seems to be the only road to travel. Rejected once too often, I cannot risk it from you. But no, I am not sick; I am torn in half and the pain is greater than I can bear alone. I need help. Oh, God, please don't let me go. Please don't let me go.

My writing filled notebook after notebook as I cried into my jack and coke, late at night, after dealing with my five children, keeping them in school and involved in all the activities of their lives.

Man is a forward-looking animal,
The future beckons me.

If I can but escape the past,
What could the present be?

~Betty Roberts

THREE

TIME

Which of us can be assured,
Can promise himself time?
Is your span so certain?
Is mine?

It is not time
That gives us cause to cry.
Consider not the 'when',
But – why?

~Betty Roberts

The Phipps Family
Grace and Bryant
Sandra Wilma Betty June

Betty P. Osborne
Real Estate Broker in Gold Coat of Century 21
State of Florida

"The Forest for the Trees"
Indian Creek Trail Madison Alabama
Oil on Canvas by Betty Roberts

Returning to nursing was again an economic necessity, and I was hired as night supervisor, so I could care for the children without help.

My oldest daughter was now a nursing student at the University of Alabama in Huntsville. The second daughter was married and had moved to Atlanta. One evening I received a call from my Dad. Mother was in the hospital and they couldn't determine what was wrong. Could I come? Leaving the younger children in the care of their oldest sister, I drove alone to West Virginia, checked Mom out of the hospital and drove her back to Alabama; Dad followed in his own station wagon—he didn't want to be "stuck" in case he decided to come back home.

It didn't take but a few days in the hospital for the diagnosis, and it was not good. Mom had Lymphoma. She began radiation and chemo, Dad driving her to her treatments so I could sleep as I was back on night duty. Mom came to me in January, and in March Dad went back home and sold all of his cattle. Mom went with him, wanting to see the farm one more time, and in a week they were back with me as she resumed her treatment. She died in August.

GRACE

Now it is over. The dreaded, long-expected ordeal is past. I am numb. Fifty baskets of flowers, an average of two hundred persons commemorated her passing with flowers, roses dew opened and drying, lilies with suffocating fragrance, decaying, ferns shredding, leaves wilted now with the August heat. Fifty baskets, most made of lard buckets spray-painted white, thrown down, tilted on the new dug ground, to cover the brown earth, the torn sod flung wide when dug, replaced haphazardly beneath the wilted flowers. Fifty outlandish garish displays of waste and thoughtfulness misplaced, memory being what it was, fond and reverent, awed with her going, unheedful of those needing her, those left behind. Careless, unthoughtful, irreverent death, rude and unkind.

She left four daughters, fifteen grandchildren, two great-grandchildren, and a young, somewhat energetic seventy-seven- year young husband. A husband with a white fringe of hair around a brown bald head, browned in the sun while cutting grass and weeding tomatoes and feeding dogs. Once he'd fed white-faced Herefords, who roamed easy, slow-footed over the same worn trails in cow pastures without fences or rails, trailing from barn to river, the herd fat full-fed, gentle with their occasional bawling.

Now he fed the anxious pups instead. Cattle gone, sold to seek help during her illness with no cure, only experimentation, trial and error, awful, careless errors. No help could be found. Too late. Too late with chemicals vein injected, suffered through and pain of home sickness for both of them, the grass turning green with early spring rains, tall and heavy with summer sun, the bald head browned during the hay cutting through the day, came bowed beside her bed at night. What can I do, he'd ask, and eyes full of pain she answered only briefly with a wisp of expression, a small drift of recognition, and then returned to a world apart, away from the grazing placid cattle and full fields of white daisies and wine clover and the bloom of goldenrod, she who loved flowers, she faded visibly, hourly before his eyes, and she passes.

And yet, she speaks, in the small movement of a grandchild, the silhouette of a daughter, the memories recalled by a friend, the bloom of a smile, a single lily rising from the mown grass, bladeless and brown colored, different, one of a kind, native to north America, a rare specific genre`, and the flowers die. The lily falls, the fifty baskets are carted away, the pale green grass begins to cover the dark earth square: what will he do without her?

Long, lonely nights. Dull, listless days. Severed in half by a loss more severe than any catastrophe to befall in his seventy-seven years. What will he do?

The four daughters are gone now, in bright new cars, twenty miles to the gallon, matched luggage, camper stocked and comfortable, grandchildren affluent, exchanging flight schedules and college addresses, and boarding planes nonchalantly while he who fears to fly sits sweatered in a wooden chair upon a patio made by laying brick . She had squatted awkwardly, a full forty figure, insisted she wanted to do it, just a hobby, all the hard work, they couldn't afford a brick layer. A herringbone pattern, she called it, chicken-scratching pattern, he'd teased, and she had laughed.

The family gone now, evaporated with countless pots of coffee, endless cakes baked by country neighbors, brown beans and cornbread sticks —how else feed such a crowd? Extra beds are put away, paper plates burned.

Now the sun has dropped below the wooded hills. The night slips into the valley, easy, quiet, still. Small sounds begin to ease into the senses. The call of the night birds, the cicadas change their high-pitched whine into a murmur, a whippoorwill cries; miles away a car moves on the distant highway. Darkness curls around the barn and a neighbor's cow moans low.

"Have to get some more cows, Grace," he says aloud. "Place will grow up come spring, if I don't."

My son and his girlfriend were married during the next summer, less than two years later the third daughter married, leaving me with one child at home. During the winter I made a trip home to see about Dad and found him snowed in, out of coal for the furnace, and staying in bed with an electric blanket to keep him warm.

"What were you planning to do if you lost power?" I asked. With his boyish, lop-sided grin, and a quick duck of his head, he laughed sheepishly. "Pull up another dog," he said. "Well, this is a three-dog night and you only have two dogs," I replied.

With no further discussion, we packed his clothes, emptied the refrigerator, locked the doors, and drove back to Alabama with the dogs. Shortly after this, Dad and I moved to Florida and bought a house together in the same neighborhood as my older sister and her husband.

By necessity, I returned to Nursing but this time, thanks to my years of experience, I found a day shift opening as supervisor of the surgical floor. The plan was for me to join my sister and brother-in-law in their Century 21 Real Estate office, but Florida law required one year's residency before you were allowed to take the examination. I started classes immediately, and in eighteen months was licensed and could leave the nursing field again, trading a forty hour a week job with every other weekend off and a steady paycheck for one with sixty hours a week, no weekends off, and an uncertain pay check. My title now, Ms. Betty Osborne, Broker - Realtor. But it was new, a real challenge, and I was out of nursing.

The real estate field presented me with new material for my writing and I was able to attend a writer's workshop on the beach at Melbourne, with the highly respected James Dickey. The three days were food for my soul.

BEGINNER'S LUCK

The bell jingled as he opened the office door, and Karen, looking up from her desk, had a vision of a Spanish matador— gleaming white shirt with wide flowing sleeves, red cape held by golden cords, black knee britches and white stockings – but in truth, the young man wore a white dress shirt and dark pants. There was a glimmer of a gold chain at his throat, but the quick black eyes and wide white smile were brighter. He offered his hand as he spoke softly.

"Habla Espanol?"

At her questioning expression, he rushed on, "Never mind, I have the English. I have only one momento and I need information."

"Certainly," replied Karen, aware that he was still holding her hand and finding it very pleasant. "How may I help you?"

"You have a sign, eight miles off the main road going south, a large house, red roof? A barn for the horses? And fenced, fenced all around? What is the price? How much land —can you tell me?"

Karen immediately placed the property as the Manzel ranch, Manzel Mansion, the real estate agents had dubbed it because of its elegance. This man was so young; she wondered if he would have the resources for such a property. Listed only a few weeks ago, by Pete, a schoolteacher who turned to real estate on weekends to supplement his teachers pay, it was the pride of the office and had been featured on last week's caravan of homes. Karen was anxious to show the prized listing.

"Please be seated, Mr. - - - -?" she said, extricating her hand. "I am sure we have the information on that property."

He caught sight of the Valu-Vista photographs displayed on the wall. "Here! Here is the house!" His face glowed as he recognized the pictures.

Karen's newly acquired real estate training came uppermost: Never disclose the price until you make an appointment to show the property. But the young man insisted, speaking urgently, "Please! I have only a few moments. I must get to the airport immediately! Please, give me the price!"

"I'll write it down for you," said Karen. He sat lightly on the edge of the chair, ready to dance away. She took a business card from her pocket, turned it over and wrote: Number 5 Deerfield Road, 9 room house, stable, ten acres, $300,000.oo.

He absorbed the information quickly with no change in expression, slipped the card into his shirt pocket. She could not bear for him to leave so quickly---making her first real state sale did not enter her mind even though the high-priced property would be the answer to her prayers. It was the man who disturbed her senses, not the sale. There was a faint, tantalizing fragrance, a sweet, delicate odor that stirred her, but he moved lightly to the door. "I will be back in two weeks," he told her, and he was gone.

Her hand still felt the pressure of his, her breath came a little faster. Going to the door she watched as he got into a large rental car with two other men as dark and as handsome as he. Judy, the receptionist, came to stand beside her.

"Judy, did you see him?"

"Ooh, whee! Did I see him!" said Judy. Karen looked at the slip of paper he had given her. Alonzo De Fuentes Sanchez. She repeated it aloud, almost like a song." Alonzo De Fuentes Sanchez" and then— "Oh! Darn! I forgot to get an address or telephone number! I can't contact him!"

"Don't feel too badly," said Judy with her usual mother-hen attitude, "It takes a while to learn all the tricks of the trade."

Judy was well-trained having been receptionist for several years. She was short, blonde, petite, and wore make-up that made her look much older. "Come on, I'll make fresh coffee," she said.

On Thursday, T.M. Drews and Karen shared floor duty. T.M. had a three o'clock closing at Southern Title Company. As he started for the door, the phone rang. "It's all yours, Karen-Baby, I'm off to get my money!"

Karen answered the phone. "How much is that mobile home you have on Kaley Drive?"

"Just one moment," said Karen, stalling for time, and Judy whispered, "What are you looking for?" Karen told her; this could be a serious buyer. "May I ask who is calling?" said Karen.

"This is Bertha Cooper." Karen inquired if Mrs. Cooper would like to see the home, and Mrs. Cooper responded, "Sure! That's why I'm calling!"

"Would this evening be convenient for you"? asked Karen, "or would tomorrow morning be better?" (Real Estate law one, Keep the conversation going until you could make an appointment. "I'm off at five," Mrs. Cooper said, "I guess this evening would do."

Only after Mrs. Cooper had hung up did Karen realize she had not obtained either an address or a phone number. With Judy's help she located the mobile home address and signed out the keys.

Mrs. Cooper looked the mobile home over carefully. "Could we show it to Bill in the morning?" she asked, and Karen quickly agreed, this time remembering to get all the vital information.

Karen had gone to the real estate convention with a new friend, Alice, who was determined to get the new widow out and circulating. It was at the convention that she had met Bert. It started as a joke, something clever to say while they were dancing. Bert had leaned down intimately, his grey eyes laughing, his body firm against hers. "You get your state license, and make three sales all by yourself, do the closing and all, and we'll get married and open an office together. I'll be the Broker, and you will be my Super-Saleswoman!"

"Why three? Is there something magic about the number three?" she had asked.

"If you can make three sales, you can make four, five.."

"I get the picture!" Karen had answered. Now, as she closed the door to the mobile home, she thought of Bert, relished the thought of calling him, dignified, polished Bert in his light gray suit and Board of Realtors tie tac. Bert, who shook hands with exactly the right amount of pressure, laughed with exactly the right amount of amused inflection. She had enjoyed his attention at the convention; she might enjoy seeing him again.

No one had told her about the early morning fog out in the county and the road was an invisible path through billowing ground clouds. The windshield wipers worked as if in a heavy rain, and thirty miles an hour was the best she could do. She would be late. It was nearly seven when she arrived.

"I've seen the outside," said Bill Cooper, "you are late."

"I'm sorry, folks! I had no idea about this fog!"

"You are not from around here." Statement, not q question, from Bill Cooper. She explained, chattering about her northern home, Tom's death, her decision to relocate and make a new career for herself. Too late, she realized she had revealed that this would be her first sale.

Bill Cooper let it pass. "We'll give $21,000 for this place," he said. "If the owner will take that, you've got yourself a sale."

"Fine, Mr. Cooper, Now, if you and Mrs. Cooper will just give me a few minutes, let me get that all down –"

"We don't have time for the paperwork now, "said Mr. Cooper, "I'll be late for work." Mr. Cooper started for the door.

"Sorry, Little lady".

"I'm sorry, too, Mr. Cooper. Real Estate law won't let us take verbal offers to the seller; it has to be in writing and signed by the buyers." Mrs. Cooper picked up the prepared contract. "Oh, come on, Bill! You've been late before! She's got it all ready."

Bill quickly scrawled his name and left for work, leaving Karen and Mrs. Cooper to lock up. "If they think the offer is too low, call me," said Mrs. Cooper. "I'll talk to Bill and we'll come up with something." Now she knew she had her first sale!

She thought about Bert, but immediately the image of Alonzo De Fuentes Sanchez came into her mind. He had said he would be back in two weeks. She recalled the faint, spicy aroma that had been Alonzo, something about the fresh morning air out in the county . . ..

Saturday morning the clock alarmed at six and Karen turned over, groaning with pain: her feet and legs ached from going door to door yesterday, Hi, my name is Karen, I am new to the neighborhood and new to Real Estate, and I would just like to get acquainted ....Thank goodness she didn't have to do that every day! It had been difficult to make her goal of fifty calls, but she had done it. She showered and dressed in her Gold career apparel, scanned the Saturday Home section of the paper, the interest rates remained unchanged. She was to meet the Hortons at nine.

Prequalified and knowledgeable, the Hortons were a young married couple renting a condo and their lease was about to expire. They had decided to buy and had been given to her by her broker. Seven hours later, out fifteen dollars for lunch and a tank full of gas, she dropped the Hortons off at their condo. There had been something wrong with every house she had shown them.

All day, and no results . . . and Saturday night alone. She was too old to cry, too young to spend Saturday night alone: she did both.

Karen slept twelve hours and Sunday morning looked bright again. As she entered her apartment after Church, her phone was ringing. "Karen White?"

"Yes? May I ask who is calling?"

"This is Homer Wilhelm. You came by my house Friday and gave me one of your cards. Do you remember me?"

She had made fifty calls on Friday —which one was he?

"How may I help you, Mr. Wilhelm?" she asked, evading his question. "I want you to sell my house. If you come out today, you can list it." Her first listing appointment!

"I can be there within the hour, Mr. Wilhelm," she said.

She thought about calling her Broker, but she knew they always took the boat out on Sunday afternoons. She would try it alone. When she left, two hours later, she carried a bag of fresh tomatoes from the back garden, and yellow roses from the front. The listing had gone smoothly, presented to Mr. Wilhelm and his son, a taller version of his Dad. The son had all the paperwork needed, the mortgage, a diagram showing room measurements.

All the articles she had read about attacks on female agents came to mind, but neither man stepped out of his courteous role.

Home again, she put the flowers in a cut glass vase, and the tomatoes in the refrigerator; she had just started to change clothes when the phone rang.

"Karen! How are you?"

It was Bert. She hadn't heard from him since the convention. "Made your first sale?" he asked.

"Yes, as a matter of fact, I have," she replied. She didn't elaborate. After a moment, Bert said, "Karen? Are you there?"

"Yes, Bert, I'm just tired. I just did a listing, and just got home."

"A listing on a Sunday? Wow! I knew you were a little ball of fire when I met you! Well, you get some rest, now, and remember, when you make that third sale, call me, and we'll go out and celebrate. That's where it's at, honey, if you can close."

On Monday morning Karen dressed carefully, brown skirt, gold and beige blouse, and the standard gold jacket. All associates were required to attend the Monday morning sales meeting held for the purpose of information and education. They met in the conference room, Mr. Taylor at the head of the large walnut table, coffee at his elbow. He went around the table for progress reports from each agent. When it was Karen's turn, she said, "I got a call yesterday, in response to the calls I made on Friday, and I listed a house."

"Tell us about it," said Mr. Taylor. Karen, with papers before her, gave all the standard details, a 3-2, square footage, details, price, and condition, appliances, etc."

"That sounds good, really good," said Mr. Taylor. "And the address?"

"One-fifty-two Butler," she replied. There was a sudden silence around the table. The agents were looking at each other. Finally, Alice said, "Is that property owned by a Mr. Wilhelm?"

"Why, yes, it is," said Karen, "He and his son."

"Oh, No! You didn't!" Again, there was silence.

"Did you meet the son, Roger?"

"Yes, I did. He was very helpful." Karen replied. Again, there was silence, then suddenly everyone burst out laughing. "We should have warned her! Why didn't someone tell her?"

"I don't understand," said Karen, confused. "Honey, that old man and his wacky son do that with every new agent. They just like to have an agent spend time with them, then the next day, they call up and cancel the listing. We've all been hooked by them -- just put it down to experience, how to do a listing, a training session, and don't let it get to you when they call up and cancel it!"

"Oh, no!" said Karen, "You are wrong! They want to sell, they want to buy a house on five acres, so they can have a larger garden!"

Mr. Taylor took control of the meeting. "Anybody else have a new listing?" The meeting was adjourned, and Judy entered the room. "I have a message for you," she said to Mr. Taylor. "Do you know a Mr. Wilhelm? Well, his wife is in England and she won't give him permission to sell the house.

He wants to cancel the listing."

Karen sat down abruptly. "I don't understand why they went through such a charade yesterday, then cancel it today!"

"Karen, didn't you feel something was wrong yesterday?" Wasn't there something not on the level? Didn't your instinct tell you something was not quite right?"

"Well, yes, there was something, . . .I half expected rape, but then, they were so nice!"

"Now do you see why we want someone with you when you make a call?" Karen tossed the listing contract on the table and

walked out. "Go after her, Judy, she's upset," said Mr. Taylor. But Karen walked out of the office and went home.

There was an iridescent dragonfly on the patio; it vacillated between the wire supporting the TV antenna and the green wrought-iron chair. Its body was blue, the net-veined wings were outlined against a sweet azure sky. She sat wrapped in her old red robe, feet tucked under, trying to make herself as small as she felt. She had gone to work feeling confident, professional, presenting her first listing, going to set the real estate world on fire. Why did she think she could succeed, when so many had failed? She was a novice, a gullible dunderhead.

Before Tom died, whenever she was blue or had a problem, he would take the opposite view, countering every negative with a positive. That was one advantage to being married but being single meant bringing yourself out of the blues.

The dragonfly jerked from the wire to the chair, erratic, hovering momentarily over the red robe over her knees. That's the way I have been ever since Tom's death, darting from one thing to another. She made up her mind: she wouldn't quit. She would stay with real estate.

Wednesday morning Karen awoke early. Her first thought was of Alonzo. It had been one week today. Only one more week to go. She lay in bed, thinking about him, his warm handclasp, his spicy smell, his flash of a smile. Would he come back next Wednesday? She jumped out of bed and dressed for work. It was her day for Floor Duty.

Shortly after one o'clock, a striking couple with 'married' written all over them, came into the office; they were dressed in matching golfing outfits of light blue and he had magnificent white hair, very full, for a man of sixty, while that of his wife was nearly as snowy, carefully beauty-parlor waved and set.

Both were tanned, energetic in their movements and had retired military stamped on them. Karen mentally classified them as she greeted them, retired, looking for a two bedroom on the golf course. She was right.

"We are the Burtons," he said," Frank and Frances, we saw a sign, near the sixteenth hole, I believe, Par Drive, and we would like to know the price."

Karen seated them, read the details on the house from the multiple listing book.

"How much?" asked Mr. Burton. Karen thought of Alonzo. When she gave him the price, he had left. She didn't want to lose these clients. "The price?" Mr. Burton insisted.

"$69,000." Karen answered. Some day she would learn more finesse, but for now the truth —and quickly—seemed the best tactic. "Let's see it," said Mr. Burton, moving toward the door, his spouse right behind him.

At the property, Mrs. Burton took charge, rushing through the rooms, verbally placing furniture, hanging drapes, making it her own. Karen followed quietly behind.

"Let's go," said Mr. Burton, completing a brief inspection. He opened the door and a sharp gust of wind swept through the empty house. Mrs. Burton caught at her hair, much as if she wore a hat. Why, that's it! It's a wig! That poor woman is wearing a wig, to compete with her husband's beautiful, natural hair. Suddenly, Karen wanted this lady to have this house: she had earned it.

"Let's get our paperwork done so you can move in," said Karen. Neither of the dignified individuals objected as she took over, but, once the details of the transaction were complete, Mrs. Burton relaxed and talked comfortably, asking Karen about herself. As Karen explained that she was a widow, she watched the blank expressions, the usual bumbled effort to recoup followed by the possessive look towards her husband, which she had encountered so many times from married women. She laughed, trying to ease the tension her widowhood had caused. "I'll have lots of ways to use my commission!" she said.

Karen and Mr. Taylor stood at the door, watching the attractive couple leave. Karen laughed softly. "What is so amusing? "asked Mr. Taylor.

"I just made my second sale, and I didn't do anything!"

"Keep it up and you will be a million- dollar producer before the next convention," said Mr. Taylor, smiling with her.

Convention. Bert. She had promised to call him. Maybe she would, maybe he would come for the weekend. She could use a break. But no, he seemed to think she had to prove herself before he would be interested in her. This was only two sales —he had said three.

Opportunity time, or Floor Duty, whichever it was called, was only available once a week because the agency had so many agents. The next week, on Wednesday, Karen dressed especially carefully, knowing she was dressing for Alonzo's return. She spent the entire day in the office, but he did not come. She went home late, undressed, and went to bed early. The sadness she felt was too deep to share, to lonely to be looked at closely even by herself.

She heard from Bert again; somehow, he had heard of her second sale and he called her. She remained noncommittal.

It was Wednesday again; the days had settled into a routine, up and dressed in career apparel, make a minimum of five telephone calls per day, arriving at the office no later than ten o'clock,, collecting mail and messages, This morning she was dressed for knocking on doors again, wearing low, comfortable walking shoes. She greeted Judy who was at the reception desk as usual. "Good morning, anything happening?"

"Oh, Karen, the Title company called about the Cooper closing. You are going to have a paycheck! Will two o'clock tomorrow be all right?"

"I don't think Mr. Cooper will want to take off work that early if he doesn't have to, could you try for four, or four-thirty?" said Karen.

"Sure, honey, I'll give it a try! "responded Judy.

The doorbell tinkled, and he was standing beside her, at the receptionist's desk. Same white dress shirt, still holding the brilliance of the sun, same aura and same faint spicy fragrance. Karen felt unsteady: she had thought too much about him to be comfortable with him now. She could not trust herself to speak, but Alonzo had no hesitation. "Here you are, Miss White!" He took both of her hands in his, held them, "We were delayed, so much to do, so many problems, when making such a big change."

He turned to the photographs on the wall. "It has not sold. It is still available? Yes?"

"It is still available," Karen said shakily.

"Come and meet my friends," and he led her to the door where three men stood. "I have told them all about you!"

"Is la Senorita Waite. Ella esta aqui, como diso que iba a Estar."

One of the men stood out because of his exceptional height and build: Karen thought he looked like a football player. Another one was older, slightly bald at the temples, paunchy around the waist, and carried a green bank courier bag under his arm. The third man, about Alonzo's age, and nearly as handsome, stood back from the others, his eyes quietly searching Karen's face, inquisitive, knowing.

She could hear the conversation taking place at Judy's desk, even as Alonzo introduced her to his friends.

"I'm up first, Judy. They are supposed to be my clients."

"They didn't ask for you, T.M. They have been here before. They are Karen's."

"How could they be? I've been on floor duty with her every day she's been here, and I haven't seen them before." Insisted T.M.

"What are they interested in, Judy?" asked Alice.

"Manzel Mansion", answered Judy.

"My God!" T.M. struck his forehead with the palm of his hand. "What a time for Mr. Taylor to be out of town!"

"The best listing in the house!" muttered Alice. "Talk about Beginner's Luck!"

At the door, Alonzo was speaking, "Miss White, this is Mr. Perez. He is from Caracas? You know? Venezuela? You know? South America?"

Karen nodded her understanding. "What did you say to him?" she asked. "Just that you are here, as you said you would be."

"Nosotros veremosla casa amora," he said to his friends, and to Karen, "We will see the house now."

Karen was calm for the situation to be so odd, so unexpected that she couldn't take it seriously. She went to the break room to get the keys to the house. Suddenly, it became very serious! She was getting ready to show a $300,000. house: the other associates were watching; it was important she handle it right. She couldn't go out in the country with four strange men, alone, to a vacant house!

"T.M. Please go with me, I have a chance to show the Manzel Mansion."

"Aren't they supposed to be my clients anyway, Karen? I'm first up."

"I gave Alonzo information on that house a month ago, T.M., and I've been waiting for him to come back!" Oh, how she'd been waiting!

Alice looked at her keenly. "You'd better go along, T.M." she said, "I'll cover for you. Karen is bound to try it."

Alonzo rode with Karen and T.M., the others following in their rental limousine. Later Alonzo would tease her, telling her he thought T.M. was her bodyguard, just as the big man was his.

Manzel Mansion was an elegant country home, red tile roof, a full acre for the front lawn, shaded by old oak trees. A screened pool adjoining the slate patio with a side veranda, five separate bedrooms, each with its own bath. An outside entrance to the veranda was an excellent feature, as was the large den with mahogany beams and a stone fireplace. The living room was highlighted with an enormous, beveled mirror, and the dining room was dominated by an antique cut-glass chandelier. The walls were dark, and a wide over-hanging eave made the interior dim and cool.

The house had been vacant for some time. Mud daubers and wasps made their clay homes under the eaves, the brown, dried grass was waist high, and there were cattle in the adjoining field, black angus, and white-faced Herefords. It was quiet, sleepy-like, and warm, although it would be chilly when the sun went down.

Karen and Alonzo stood at the front portico; T.M. stayed with the car. The three men walked through the house, inspecting each room.

"Shouldn't we go with them?" she asked.

"No, let them be."

"Wouldn't you like to see the inside?"

"I have seen it."

"When --?"

"Before, I come here before your office."

"But inside --?"

"There was a window . . . "His voice trailed off, he gestured with a slender hand.

She could not visualize him prying open a window, crawling through like some street urchin . . . she looked at him closely. Alonzo returned her scrutinizing look steadily, unsmiling. She looked away first, breathless. "Come," she said, "lets inspect the stables with the others."

She walked some distance away, grateful for her comfortable shoes on the soft soil. The beauty of the place moved her, and she wondered how Mr. Manzel could bear to sell it. Alonzo came to stand with her.

"What is a lovely young lady like you doing in business?"

"Doing fairly well," she said with a laugh.

"In my country, you would be at home with a husband and children."

Karen waited for the pain that always came with reference to her husband, framing her stock reply, "I am a widow," but then she hesitated. Would that knowledge weaken her bargaining position? Could it change her position? Wasn't it time she stopped trading on sympathy? She quickly changed the subject.

"What does Mr. Perez think of the property?' she asked. She had learned on the drive out to the house that Mr. Perez was the actual buyer. "It is as I knew it would be," Alonzo said, which really didn't tell her anything. As they returned to the office, she noticed the parking lot was unusually full. She led the group back to a small consulting area, pulled the folding doors together, and brought in an extra chair. Karen seated herself, a notepad and pen on the glass-topped table before her. The men changed positions, then seated themselves, Alonzo in front of Karen, Mr. Perez to her right, the reticent one to her left, and the young football player took the extra chair, leaned it against the wall and sat in it, out of the way.

Karen added a contract to the note pad before her and prepared to fill it out. The office was strangely still, no typewriters or phone calls, no talking, everybody prepared to listen in to the conversation in the conference room. Her hands were shaking; she folded them together and tucked them in her lap under the table, then realized that everyone at the table could see her hands. She was going to talk to Mr. Taylor about these tables. Mr. Taylor! How she wished her Broker were here! If ever she needed professional guidance, it was now.

"Alonzo tells me you are from Caracas?" she said to Mr. Perez. Alonzo translated for her, explaining, "Mr. Perez has no English. In my country, I speak for him, I am in land exchange also, but here I have no license."

"Fine, Alonzo, let's get some details out of the way." She moved the contract forward. *"Buyer's name?"* she asked. *"You misunderstand,"* Alonzo said gently. *"We only want to talk to the owner, just to talk between men."*

"I'm sorry," she said. *"We do not take verbal offers to our clients. It must be written down and signed."* It had worked with Mr. Cooper, Karen thought, maybe it will work again. That had been a 21,000 deal—this was three hundred thousand! Alonzo spoke rapidly to Mr. Perez in their native language, and she could not follow what was being said. Suddenly, the fourth man spoke, a few terse words. Alonzo turned back to her.

"We cannot speak to the owner?"

"You speak for Mr. Perez; I speak for Mr. Manzel." From instinct, she waited for Alonzo to reply. She was acutely aware of the silence of the four men, but also of the silence in the entire office.

Alonzo looked at the fourth man, the handsome, quiet one who had taken no part in the negotiations thus far. The man nodded, said, *"Si."* Karen comprehended the go-ahead signal. She pulled the contract toward her. *"Name of the buyer?"*

"Perez, Roberto Antonio Garcia Perez."

"Address?" Alonzo replied, *"Edo Mirando 92-18, Caracas, Venezuela, South America."*

"The offer?" She held her gold pen, ready to write, trying to appear casual, as if she wrote hundred thousand dollar offers every day.

"Tell me," Alonzo said, *"would it be possible to buy additional land nearby?"*

"It might be possible," Karen hedged, not having a clue to that possibility. She knew almost nothing about plat books or what was for sale in the area. Mr. Taylor, where are you?

"What would farmland cost? Land for cattle?"

"It would depend on where it is located," she hedged again.

How could she get their signature on the contract before they realized she was stabbing in the dark?

"Give an estimate on, say, a hundred acres."

"Alonzo, I can't do that!" she protested. "If I give you a price, you will come back later and hold me to it!"

"No, no. I would not do that! I only need some suggestion for how much money we would need to bring in U. S. dollars!"

Like an inspiration, she recalled the old rule of thumb drilled into her in real estate class. "Alonzo, there's only three things that affect the price of land."

Alonzo leaned forward expectantly, "What are the three things?"

The office was quiet, everyone literally holding their breath. Karen smiled, as she leaned forward. "Location," she said, paused, and continued slowly, "Location, and location."

He looked puzzled, then leaned back in his chair and laughed, white teeth flashing. The fourth man laughed also, and Karen realized: He speaks English! Mr. Perez did not change expressions. "I told you she was smart!" cried Alonzo.

Now, she could press for an answer. "How shall we make the offer?"

Alonzo gave the answer, all at once, obviously preplanned. "We will pay forty thousand now, sixty thousand in three months, eighty thousand in six months, eighty thousand in one year. No interest."

Karen could not add the figures in her head—oh, Lord, what a time to be without scratch paper. Her heart raced in near panic. She did not dare leave the table now! She thought of her business cards, always in her jacket pocket, and pulled one out., jotting down the terms. Forty, Sixty, eighty, eighty –not full price. The total was two hundred and sixty thousand, forty thousand short, but all in one year. Would Mr. Manzel accept that?

It was her turn to hesitate. She sat looking at the card, a frown on her face. The stillness in the office deepened. The men waited. She was bound by real estate law to get the best price possible for *her seller. She couldn't argue with them, she couldn't even speak their language. She was just a messenger to them, a woman who belonged at home raising babies. She realized they would prefer not to deal with her at all. She decided she would not jeopardize the sale by trying to alter the terms. If Mr. Manzel wanted to wait for another buyer, it might take a year –this way he would have most of his money and not be asked to carry a mortgage. Perhaps he could counter, even split the difference. She looked up at Alonzo. The sale must go through.*

"We will need a binder," she said.

"How much?"

"Ten percent is usual, but since the amount is so great, how about ten percent of the first payment?"

"We will pay the usual amount," Alonzo said, and she saw the fourth man give an affirmative nod. Karen realized this was where the decisions were made. And he understood English perfectly. Now, Alonzo spoke softly to Mr. Perez, who responded by taking the green bank bag from under the table and counting out twenty-six thousand dollars, all in U. S. one hundred-dollar bills, in stacks of tens, fanning out the six separately.

Karen had never seen so much money. She could feel the perspiration trickle down between her breasts, she wet her lips and unconsciously slipped her shoe off under her chair. She had a wild, irrational urge to jump up, walk around, move, anything but sit still. But first, before she blew the whole deal, she had to get a signature on that contract. She moved the paper over, in front of Alonzo, not knowing who would actually sign it. Alonzo moved the contract around the piles of money, and Mr. Perez signed it. Alonzo witnessed it, then moved it over to the fourth man, who also witnessed it. Back again to her, she signed her name as agent. Now, all it lacked was Mr. Menzel's signature—and she had no idea when she could get in touch with him. She had to move, to take a breath, to wipe her face –anything to relieve the tension.

"I'll get in touch with Mr. Manzel immediately," she said, and picked up the piles of money.

Forgetting her shoes, she padded in to the receptionist's desk. There sat Judy, Alice, T.M. and a half dozen extra agents.

"Judy," she said, "will you count this with me? I need a receipt." Judy put her arm around her, and whispered, "You did it! I'll get your shoes.".

Karen took her clients to the Red Dragon while Pete, the listing Associate, called Mr. Manzel. Alonzo sat close beside her on a comfortable divan, his spicy aroma making her dizzy.

"Tell me about Caracas," she said as they waited for cool drinks. "It is cooler there, in the mountains. But it is over three thousand miles above the sea. We have much oil, but the people are farmers, like yours." He shook his head. "But we have much problems, my country. It is good for me to come to the United States."

The conversation continued, relaxed and comfortable. Back at the office, she found seats for her clients and joined the others in the break room.

"How are we doing?" she asked Pete.

"Mr. Manzel is out of town," he said, "I've contacted his son, he's trying to reach him now."

Alice followed her to the Ladies room. "How are you doing, Kid?"

"Scared to think about it," said Karen. "Sure wish Mr. Taylor was here."

"Judy called him—he's on his way, be here shortly."

As they came out of the ladies' room, they could hear the conversation in the break room.

". . . should have been my sale. I was first up; she hadn't worked with them before." T.M. was saying.

"That's not so, T.M. and you know it!" said Judy. "Karen met that man some time ago. He came up to her because he knew her!" The conversation stopped as they entered the room. Everyone looked

at Karen, but it was Alice who spoke. *"Really, T.M."* Then, to Karen, Alice said, *"Now you know why we call him 'T.M', don't you! Mr. "Too Much" Drewes!"*

The time passed slowly, and by four o'clock Mr. Manzel had not been located. Karen explained the problem to Alonzo. "Have your secretary call the airlines, make reservations for the eight o'clock flight to Miami, cancel the five o'clock one. Just say, reservations for Alonzo De Fuentes Sanchez and friends!" His smile took her breath away.

Mr. Taylor arrived by five and then Mr. Manzel called, and agreed to the terms, provided the agency would accept their commission in divided payments also. Mr. Taylor, Pete and Karen quickly agreed. By six-thirty everyone had congratulated everyone else several times, the staff was gone, the other associates drifted away after learning the contract had been accepted, and the office was quiet. Alonzo's three friends waited for him in the car.

"Did you think I would come again?" he asked, holding both of her hands.

"Yes, I thought you would come back," she said.

"And I will bring others from my country." They stood by the door, looking at each other seriously. "I fail to see why you do not raise a family," he said, and then he smiled, lightening the mood.

"I enjoy what I do," replied Karen, "It's rewarding, it's exciting . . ." and as she said it, she realized it was true. She thought of Mrs. Cooper, with her geranium-red hair, and Mrs. Burton, holding on to her wig, Mr. Perez—somehow this transaction did not fit into the same frame work; each client is different, the rewards were different, too. "I'm here because I want to be," she said, with a smile. Alonzo brought her hands to his lips. "Someday a man will come, will take you out of business and care for you in the home, as a woman should be cared for." He joined his friends in the big black rental car and they were soon out of sight.

Karen stood by the door, regaining her composure slowly. She had identified the stirring, spicy aroma. It was carnations . . . high school prom night, carnations. Then she laughed. The only man interested in her at present wanted to marry her just to open an office with her, not to take her out of the business! She walked back to her desk, dropped exhausted into her chair. There was a note from Judy clipped to her calendar. She eased out of her shoes as she read:

Karen,

The Cooper closing is set for four-thirty tomorrow. Congrats, gal. You were a pro. Love, Judy

A pro. That was what she wanted to be, on her own, not in a two-man office with a man only interested in her sales ability. It was good to feel competent, professional. Maybe, someday . . . but not now. She picked up the phone.

"Mrs. Cooper? Hi, It's Karen. We are all set to close on your new home. Yes, that's right! Will four-thirty tomorrow be convenient for you and Mr. Cooper? Fine! I'll see you then!"

THE BOTTOM LINE

Yesterday was Wednesday, (a middlin' busy day, as Monday and Tuesday were slow, Thursday and Friday hectic, Saturday, impossible, and Sundays we were closed). I was in the Century 21 office, at my desk as I was assigned "floor duty". Floor duty was both a blessing and a curse: Whoever walked in was your prospect, but on the other hand, you couldn't leave, you were also the telephone operator. All you could do was paper-work and be ready to greet anyone who opened the door.

An attractive senior-citizen couple walked in, took seats, and announced, "We'd like to sell our house."

As I took the 'particulars'—lakefront, white sandy beach, lovely house with extra acreage, and only ten miles from Walt Disney World—I realized I had lucked into a realtor's dream listing: the property would sell itself. (Interested? See your agent –I will happily Co-broke!)

Friends, this is not a Real Estate commercial. There is more.

Last Sunday we were asked to fill out our Church Pledge cards for the coming year. We'd been told that our church was behind in their obligations on the general budget, and a new building was already under construction. We were being asked to increase our pledge, to give more, our commitment based on salary; but I worked on commission and never knew how much I would make. How could you pledge on an unknown figure?

As we knelt at the communion railing, I made a vow: Lord, ten percent of each check, regardless of the amount, will go toward building your Kingdom here, right here, in my hometown.

On Monday, I had accompanied my customers to the closing on their new home, the sale made weeks ago. On Tuesday, my Broker had handed me the commission check. "Congratulation," he had said.

"Thank you," I said aloud to him, but silently I said, "Thank you, Lord," For I really needed the extra income. The check looked big to me, even after deducting the ten percent, and I vowed to write the check to the church at the same time I wrote the deposit slip for the bank.

Emerson once wrote, "It is one of the most beautiful compensations of this life that no man can sincerely try to help another without helping himself."

I could rationalize my new dream-listing: These folks need my help —I would earn my commission. It was my turn for a break. It would balance out the deals I lost. But no matter how I rationalized it, there remained that promise made at the alter on Sunday. He had presented me with another opportunity even before I had paid the tithe, opened another door on the strength of my promise only! I prefer to think it was His way of reassuring me, once again, that you can't out-give the Lord.

Yes, I know, don't count your chickens before they hatch, yada-yada, the property is listed, not SOLD! But Friend, this is the bottom line: If God provided the seller, will he not also provide the buyer? Hum, now, let's see. Ten percent of one-half a million is . . .."

FOUR

NIGHT

Stillness throbs in rhythm with the heart.
No ticking of clocks with
iridescent digits glowing in the dark.

No wind or rain, storm or commotion
No tearing or shredding of the soul with strong emotion

Is it now, or yesterday
Or is it tomorrow?

Is this peace – or only freedom from sorrow?

~Betty Roberts

Betty Osborne
Student at University of Alabama in Huntsville

Betty Osborne, R.N.

"Return to Earth"
Oil on Canvas by Betty Roberts

A chance meeting between my daughter and a former classmate of mine resulted in a renewed friendship. Now divorced, he asked about me and my daughter told him about her father's death and that I had moved to Florida. He called me and we began to renew our friendship – long distance. First phone calls, then letters, then visits and 6 months later I moved back to Alabama. We were married in his home church with both families and all the kids in attendance. I acquired two more children in the bargain; a boy who was beginning high school and another daughter who was in her first year of college.

We bought a lovely home on five acres of land out in the county, and only fifteen minutes from the telephone manufacturing plant where he worked as an engineer. Again, I returned to nursing, another financial necessity, and again all I could find was night shift.

Hospital policy required all new employees to start on either 11 to 7 or 3 to 11 and they moved to day shift when a vacancy occurred, according to length of time employed in that institution, regardless of education or experience. My choice of what was available was night shift on the surgical floor, which allowed me to have evenings free to spend with my new husband and our youngest daughter who was now in high school. My hours were filled with no time or energy for my writing. Once again, my title changed to Mrs. – Mrs. Betty Roberts R.N.

My Dad, forever unhappy after giving up his farm and moving to Florida, became homesick and wanted to visit relatives in North Carolina. At the age of eighty, my sister and I tried to talk him out of it, telling him to wait until one of us could get away from work to go with him. That was an insult to him, he was perfectly able to drive by himself, and this he did. He went to a cousin's house and two male cousins took Dad to see a new Windmill just built near their home to generate electricity. Dad had spent his entire life putting up high-voltage electrical wiring to operate electric locomotives on the railroad, wiring he removed just before retiring as the electric engines gave way to diesel; the cousins knew he would be interested in the windmill.

Unfortunately, Dad never made it to the Windmill. He was sitting in the back seat of the cousin's car when he had a stroke. The cousin, recognizing he was in trouble, wheeled around and sped to the local hospital, saving Dad's life. The stroke left him paralyzed on one side and without speech. He knew what was taking place around him but was unable to communicate.

My sisters and I met in North Carolina and the next day we transferred him to Richmond, to the hospital where our younger sister worked. After a short stay in Virginia, my older sister, her husband, son and I went to Richmond and brought Dad back to his house in Florida. My husband found a new position in Florida, and we moved from Alabama. I became my Dad's caretaker, living with Dad in the house we had bought together. This lasted for several months; our contract ended, and we "bounced" back to Alabama again. It became difficult for my older sister to find caregivers for our father, so Dad was placed in a nursing facility. Over the next few months, I made several trips to Florida, usually alone because my husband was working, and my daughter was in school. The following short story reflects those long drives alone.

A COLD WIND

Martha loosened the pure silk scarf at her throat with a heavily jeweled hand. Idly, she turned the radio dial from station to station, searching for music, but preacher followed preacher with Sunday morning services based on Daniel, Ezekiel, Moses ---- why were there no sermons based on the New Testament?

She began to notice the numerous hitchhikers along the road, huddled under the concrete overpasses, brown bags at their feet, coat collars turned up against the cold wind – wind made stronger by each passing vehicle. The hitchhikers faced the traffic, arms extended, thumbs up. Wayfaring strangers, and if she were a good Samaritan, she would pick one of them up. But, no, David would not want her to do that. She tried to recall an instance in which he had given a traveler aid, but she could not. But David was not with her this time. She traveled alone for the first time. She sighted a lone figure in the distance and with no hesitation, the small car slowed, responding to an almost subconscious decision to pick up the hitchhiker.

He was walking backwards, with jerky sideways steps that allowed him a forward movement while maintaining a close look at oncoming traffic. His arm was out, thumb waving in the direction she was going. No shelter under the bridge for this one, no standing or waiting, dependent upon the whims of wheeled citizens.

She braked sharply and pulled onto the shoulder of the road, rolling to a stop before an Emergency Stopping Only sign. The wheels were hardly still before the young man slid into the front seat beside her and slammed the door.

His face, above the beard of several days, was red from the cold wind. He had narrow brows that almost touched across a nose now thinning and flaring from the hard run to the car. His long and skimpy hair was held back by a black baseball cap, remnant of some long-ago summer ball game, and faded blue denim covered a thin, shaking frame. His eyes avoided direct contact as he blew on chilled fingers, finally tucking them between his legs to warm.

"Cigarette, Lady?"

"Sorry, I don't smoke."

The young man glanced at her briefly then looked away.

Martha had been driving several hours and the warmth of the car made her forget the sharpness of the wind and the near-freezing temperatures until he had opened the door. Now the early spring sun made an uncomfortable glare, obscuring her vision, as she pulled back into traffic and resumed speed. "Where are you going?" she asked.

"Long ways."

Several miles were covered in silence. The radio gave a short news summary and a brief weather bulletin, sunny, cold, temperature 34 with a high of 37 expected today. Typical February. She had not realized it was so cold.

The young man stretched his feet toward the heater. She noticed the worn brown shoes, and, with a shock, she realized he wore no socks. His ankles were raw and chapped-looking, rubbed raw where the jeans scrapped bare skin. Certain that he was still cold, she moved the small thermos of coffee resting in the seat closer to him.

"It's still hot," she said.

He opened the bottle and drank directly from it, ignoring the small cup which doubled as a top, drank without pause for breath and when the bottle was drained, he dropped it into the seat again.

Expectantly she waited for his expression of appreciation, eager to begin a conversation. He said nothing. He sat hunched down in the seat, hands again between his thighs, peering at the road, eyes dull and unblinking. His elbows stiffened and he clasped his knees together to still their shaking. He blew out a deep breath, half sigh, half whistle, and settled into the curve of the seat. The long hours in the cold and in the wind had required a tension that was almost impossible to maintain and now he gave in to the soft seat, his arms went limp, his thighs fell outward as he hooked his thumbs in the downward slits of his pockets. Slowly the warmth of the car penetrated the faded jeans and jacket.

As he clearly relaxed, she searched for questions to relieve the silence.

"Are you from around here?"

"No."

"How far are you going?"

"Long ways."

"Job hunting?"

"Was—didn't find nothin'".

"What work do you do?"

"Anything."

"I meant, what did you take in school? Did you go to college, or trade school?" she persisted.

"No," he said shortly.

"What is your name?"

"John."

She waited a long moment, then volunteered, "I'm Mrs. Norton." He did not comment, and the conversation was again ended.

She drove rapidly, taking a by-pass around a small city, moving again into interstate traffic without decreasing speed, into open country over hills scared by the twisting highway, along unmarked lanes of sameness, unrelieved from state to state, with overhead exchanges and gasoline signs on high poles piercing the sky. The light, new green of spring faint in the fields and outlining the branches of trees still dark with the wetness of winter, gave an eerie silence to the world beyond the plate-glass windows, except for the zip of cars and the more solid whoosh of trucks. The deadening, dull motion of the car numbed her senses and began to threaten her attentiveness. She had not anticipated the lengthening of the route when unbroken by conversation—David had always been such a talker—nor the slowness of time unmarked by interruption. She had picked up this young man to provide some relief from the boredom—and now he sat silent and withdrawn.

David would not have approved of her action, and she decided not to tell him, but it would make a good story to tell at the club, how she had befriended a poor boy, one out of work and cold . . . why, she'd say, he didn't even have on socks! David would think her reckless and foolish, the way he always locks up everything and reads the stories in the local paper about robberies, the murders . . . she glanced at the boy beside her. At the moment he seemed harmless enough, still. . ..

"Would you like to turn the radio up?" she asked.

There was no reply. She reached over, turned the dial for some moments, finally located a clear station, with the announcer in the midst of a commercial. "Let's leave it at this for a while, perhaps there will be music."

She tried again, "Do you like country music? That's all that has been on today, that and preaching. Do you go to church?"

"No," he said. He leaned back against the seat and released his seat belt, stared at the roof of the little car, seeming oblivious to both her and his surroundings for now the straight highway was gone and they wound into low foothills with a gradually increasing altitude.

Martha wondered if the "No" applied to her question about the music, or about the church but decided not to press it. "Certainly, are a number of hitchhikers today," she commented. "I wouldn't have thought people would be thumbing on a Sunday."

He turned to her with a curious look on his face. "What has Sunday got to do with it?" he asked.

She laughed, somewhat startled by his question. "Well, you know, it's rather a family day . . . "

She searched for a way to explain her statement. "Church and all . . .."

He turned away from her and looked out the window.

A talk show had started on the radio: "New product, developed by the Coca-Cola co., could be distributed through the public schools if it were approved.

"Do you have a family?" she asked.

He moved away, a small gesture, a quick negative shake of the head. "No family to speak of," he said.

"My husband works for the Space Program," she volunteered. "It's very hard for him to get away . . . '

"New product is called Samson," continued the radio, "and provides all the protein needed for a growing child in just one cupful a day."

"This is the first time I've made this trip alone." She said. "The Department of Agriculture has turned thumbs down on the product", the commentator continued, "Butz is playing politics."

"Oh, everyone plays politics," she commented, suddenly caught by the direction the talk was taking. The program began to annoy her. "David says so, all the time."

The radio continued. "Samson would interfere with the free milk program and dairy farmers are lobbying against it."

She opened her mouth indignantly to protest, but a sideways glance at her young passenger with his thin face stopped her. She knew he was listening to the program also. What did he think of a governmental decision to let children go undernourished? But he probably didn't even vote. What was his world like? Where did he sleep at night? What did he eat? Suddenly she realized he was probably hungry right now. If he were, and if he had no money —she reached, instinctively, for her purse lying on the seat beside her, opened it nonchalantly, removed a lace-trimmed handkerchief and touched the corners of her mouth. She replaced the handkerchief, but left the purse lying in her lap.

The boy glanced at her briefly then turned back to the window.

Why did he look at her? She tried to think of something to break the strained silence, but she could not. The radio blared now with a male quartet singing "Steel Away, steel away, Jesus," and angrily she snapped it off. The stillness was just as bad. Her hands gripped the steering wheel and she felt the tension along her spine, felt it move through her knees, causing the muscles in her calves to tighten, her foot pressed more firmly on the accelerator and she increased the speed, sixty, seventy, seventy-five, she began looking for signs along the way, seeking a means to terminate the uncomfortable association. She began passing cars, then the camper-trucks which were numerous, gradually challenging the tractor-trailers and their accompanying high winds. The small car swayed and bounced, she clung to the wheel, steadying its roll.

The young man sat relaxed, his long frame adjusted to the curving seat as he rode with the motion of the car as one accustomed to danger and to speed. There seemed to be no intersections along this part of the interstate, but she quickly tired of the effort required to keep the car under control and gradually slowed to normal speed.

For several miles she searched for something to say, forming near-apologies, I'm so sorry I picked you up, I'm so sorry it occurred to me you might steal from my purse, I'm so sorry you can't talk to me, I'm so sorry I picked you up in the first place—but the silence stretched out unbroken.

Finally. An Exit sign. Food. Gas. Phone. Lodging. She pulled into the turn-off lane. "I want to stop for a while," she said. "Do you want off here or in the town?"

"I've no money for a restaurant," he said. "I'll get off here."

The cold wind jerked the car door from his hand when he opened it, and he grabbed it, slammed it harder than necessary. He began walking. There was no Thank You, and he did not look back.

Quickly she drove up the slope to the side road. Thank God! That is that! If only he had talked to me or been somewhat civil!

He was like so many of those young people at church. They used to talk to her, but now, with this long-hair and blue-jean craze, their attitude had changed over the years.

She parked in front of a large, auspicious hotel and chose a small table by the window. She ordered crisp bacon, eggs easy over, biscuits with honey, not the usual cheap packets of jam. She placed a linen napkin over her silk-covered knees and sipped hot coffee. His face blurred before her, became the face of countless youths, over the years, some of whom once had been close to her, substitutes, compensation for the children she never had, receivers of frustrated affection. . ..

She shook her head. Someone would pick him up, besides, he wasn't even friendly. He would just have to learn; you can't go through life ignoring the rest of the world. And then it occurred to her: Did the Good Samaritan really go back to that Inn on the Jericho Road? There was no record of the return trip.

She ate slowly while cars flowed past on the interstate below. She generously tipped the young waitress, common in her blue skirt and white pinafore, blonde hair tied back, chipped nail polish on stubby ungraceful fingers. She smiled graciously at the gushing thanks. What a pleasant young lady.

She followed the long, curving access road and eased into the faster flowing interstate traffic. Conscious of her time delayed, the long wait to be served, fretful over the long distance yet to be traveled, she began to pick up speed. She topped a slight rise in the road and immediately recognized the figure ahead.

The car seemed to hang suspended in a moment of time, motionless, seeming to maintain the distance between them for an eternity, unchanged, unmoved. What could she say to him if she stopped again?

She saw his bent head and felt with him the cold wind that fanned him. She saw the outstretched arm, the crooked thumb held up. She saw the white skin of ankles, bare above the brown shoes that slipped up and down over rough heels with each backward step, walking, walking, even while he searched for a ride.

Now she was close to him, almost beside him—perhaps he hadn't seen her —yes, he had, he recognized her. For a moment she panicked, her foot jerked convulsively on the gas pedal as if it were going to slow up. The ball cap was pushed back, holding the stringy hair out of his face but the wind whipped its length out behind him and it waved in rhythm with the passing cars; the jeans flapped against thin legs in the cold wind.

Now she could see his face. She saw his young lips twist as their eyes met in one quick glance, then he turned his head, sharply, deliberately, away from her to the pale green fields beyond the road. She saw his arm jerk down, the thumb tuck into the palm, as he turned a thin blue shoulder in her direction. And kept on walking.

From the date of his first stroke, Dad had several months of relatively good health. He never regained his ability to talk, except with single words, head nods, and smiles, but he was able to communicate by gestures and his one-word vocabulary, which was, "see". If he became agitated, or frustrated because we didn't understand, he would say, "see, see, see, "and keep on saying it, pointing, until it was clear to us. Then he would relax and laugh, nod his head, and sometimes get tears in his eyes.

At one point, he became very ill, and I made an extended trip back to help with his care. He had fallen, fractured a hip, and required surgery. Following surgery, his kidneys shut down, total renal failure, and we didn't expect him to survive. The following story is almost as much fact as fiction.

DIARY OF A DIET

March 28 – Day One

7 a.m. Breakfast: Black coffee. Two large white grapefruit (200 calories) very sweet and delicious, Florida's best.

12 Noon: One cup 2% milk (130 calories) with a vitamin and mineral tablet. I must remember to buy calcium tablets too. One medium apple (60 calories). Apple was too green and hard, not satisfying, left me feeling hungry and mistreated.

4 p.m. Resisted temptation to buy ice cream with Amy. Her diminutive figure will tolerate praline cream—mine won't. Took one bite of hers then concentrated on my shopping. Felt good about not eating ice cream.

5 p.m. Very hungry and slight headache. Need to eat but must stay at hospital with Dad until his tray comes—he cannot eat without help –then home to cook for Ray and Amy.

Supper plan: Fish Pattie (200) Broccoli (20) Diet bread (40) with orange marmalade (20). Total: 280.

Actual Intake: All of the above, plus Diet bar (200) bought for tomorrow's lunch, four Ayds (100) and a full pot of black coffee.

Today's total:840
Exercise: Bike ride 30 minutes.

Mental attitude: Depression is somewhat lifted; dieting is an attempt at self-discipline that makes me feel better.

Dad's condition seems to be deteriorating. Urine output for the twenty-four hours is less than 200cc's; the edema seems to be increasing. Have not told my family yet. Hospital personnel know that I am with him and know I am a nurse; they seldom come in the room. I do all the turning and cleaning, trying to save them the time and trouble. Since the stroke two years ago he has been helpless, aphasia and right-side paralysis. He is not in good spirits today; I cannot leave him alone. The chairs in this room are straight-backed, the cushions stiff. It will be another long night.

March 29—Day Two

Dad rolled and turned every thirty minutes last night from 1a.m. until 6a.m. By daylight I was worn out and he was asleep. Home at nine-thirty. No interest in Breakfast, too much coffee during the night.

Exercise: Bike ride 30 minutes.
Weight Loss: Three pounds. Encouraging.

10 a.m. Unable to sleep, up and ate two pink grapefruit, seeded. Very good and cold. In the mood for sex but Ray is at the office, as usual.

3 p.m. Slept soundly until Amy came from school. Not at all hungry. Back to hospital to relieve Aunt Margaret. Dad has had a bad day, she says, nausea and diarrhea, the edema is increasing, less than fifty cc's of urine output since midnight.

6 pm. Supper: Two hard-boiled eggs, brought from home (150) and more coffee. No salt. Too tired to walk down the hall to get it and forgot to bring it. Sent Dad's tray back, untouched. Ray is here, watching T.V. until the news and weather report ends, then goes home. Bea stops by on her way home from the office. It is obvious we are sisters, physically alike, short, stocky, inclined to being overweight like Mother, but there the similarity ends for Bea is business oriented, precise, impeccable, promptly at her desk at nine a.m. and busy all day; she has little free time. I share my concern regarding the low output; she needs no medical background to comprehend the gravity of this complication.

After Bea leaves, I wish Ray had stayed. He cannot tolerate the hospital; does not realize how badly I need someone to talk to me. All Dad can say is, "see, see", the only word left him since his stroke. There is nothing more confining to a nurse who is accustomed to working all over the building, as staying in one single, small room, by one bed with one patient, even if he is my father. I do not feel the support of anyone at this hour. The television light bothers Dad; I have read for hours. Everything revolves around this room, a microcosm; the only thing more isolating than being a nurse in street clothes doing private duty is a nurse who is the patient: other nurses tend to avoid one, in either case. I nibble on wheat crackers with cheese (138 calories per package) filched from the nourishment room along with endless cups of coffee —white, Styrofoam cups that make my lips feel dry and rough. What I wouldn't give for a china cup!

Today's total: 560.

Missed the milk and still no calcium tablets. I couldn't stand a broken hip. Poor Dad, the stroke two years ago and now a broken hip. We didn't expect the post-surgery renal shutdown; there had never been a problem with the kidneys.

Exercise schedule today was wonderful. The half-hour bike ride this morning, then at eleven tonight, during shift change, when the night nurse would be making rounds and probably would look in on Dad, I slipped out and walked two and a half miles. Why do I feel so guilty when taking thirty minutes for myself?

It was brisk and lovely, starshine made it easy to see. The moon

was not bright, like it is now, coming through the window. I found
a stick, a fallen tree limb, rough and crooked in my hands, but
comforting in case I met that Doberman again, like last time. I
tell myself that his growl is friendly and stick to my premeasured
trail—how else would I know how far I've walked?

ODE TO A STRANGE DOG

"A walk is only a stroll if there is no goal,
A wandering in the moonlight.
Not willing to negotiate I keep a steady gait
And resist the urge of flight.
His wide mouth gapping dog teeth snapping,
My heart compensates for fright."

Dad struggles to turn over. The edema has made his body so heavy
he cannot move without my help. I pull him to his side and support
his swollen legs with pillows. I think of my own legs pumping so
effortlessly over the paved road, feel the cool air on my face, the deep
breath of orange blossoms fills my lungs and I remember counting to
ten and exhaling slowly. How grand it felt! This time I know I will
make it back to my normal weight of one-twenty-five. Dear Lord, it
is four a.m. Every time I try to lie down, he calls me—the cushions
from the chair are much more comfortable on the floor. It is as
though he is afraid for me to go to sleep, lest he need me and not be
able to call.

March 30 –Day Three

Ray comes as usual at seven and Dad's tray arrives at eight. I
remove the cover, mix Sanka in tepid water with powdered creamer
that floats on top and refuses to dissolve.

Dad coughs and chokes on mucus and we all three gag. Ray tries to escape to the office and I am compelled to invite myself to breakfast with him, wanting to run from the room.

My calorie count lists waffles as 86 calories, syrup as 54; I liberally figure it at 200 and eat every bite, not missing the butter at all. I feel guilty and wonder if this is the beginning of the end; the trite phrase reminds me of another: I've only lost a minor skirmish, not the whole war. The 'sweet tooth' filled with crisp waffle and blueberry syrup, I strengthen my resolve and return to the hospital. Now guilt takes over and I give Dad his bath, not waiting for the day nurse, trying to make up for running away.

12 noon. Lunch: One diet coke, calories, zero. It has been twenty-four hours since I've slept at all. I wonder, why this frenzied diet activity? This is the most stressful time—why now? Am I punishing myself? If so, for what?

7 p.m. Thank God for dear Aunt Margaret. She is so like my mother used to be. I needed the break and slept well for a few hours. Too tired to bike ride. Supper tonight was boiled eggs again but I remembered the salt.

Today's total: 350
Weight loss: 5 pounds.

12 midnight. Discovery: At 56 degrees the whip-poor-wills are silent; at sixty degrees they sing, even in the rain. It is easy to become philosophical after walking three miles. That is one of the extraordinary facts about long, brisk walks. It is an exciting experience that has nothing to do with weight loss; the euphoria described by runners is comparable. By the end of the walk I am not thinking about Dad dying but am making plans to take him home. All negative thoughts and feelings are gone and my feet move by themselves while my mind rushes forward in joy.

On Robinson Avenue there is a livestock market with auctions each Wednesday. Evan at midnight men are still loading cattle trucks. A tractor-trailer rig pulls up to the loading dock, a big, slatted, double-decker and cattle bawl as they are driven into the upper level. The warm green smell of manure is that of the barn at home, years ago, and the feel of light rain is the mist of Bluestone River. The paved road becomes the country lane I walked as a girl. Dad never showed affection; it was unmanly in his generation. Now I feel myself pulling away from him, keeping it light, withholding my love, because it hurts. We are so much alike, brusque, comic when the situation calls for sincerity. He seemed to take his strength from the elements, working through ice storms and frying sun, walking miles of railroad track summer and winter, then home to walk again, to the river to 'check on' the cattle, or to the high place on the hill overlooking the land, sitting on the rocks beneath the ancient spruce, and taking it all in. Even now we must open the vertical blinds to let in the sunlight, or, like tonight, the moonlight. And I, like my Dad, must walk in the weather, smell the rain-wet cattle, hear the night birds and feel the glory of it all.

March 31 – Day Four

(a.m. breakfast: English muffin (130) jelly (35) one egg (100). Sleep. Ah, sleep!

Lunch: Salad at nearby Parsons Table (est. 200) no dressing on salad.

5p.m. Dad's tray had pumpkin pie on it (est.230); he would not eat it at all. I remove it from his tray. It would be my reward for staying these long hours, and, after all, todays total was only 465.

7:30 p.m. Just as I decided to eat the pumpkin pie Ray and Bea arrived, preplanned timing, to give me a change. While Bea sat with Dad, Ray and I went to a recently reopened restaurant and waited too long, to eat too much, with poor service and exorbitant prices. We determined that our only recreation was going out to eat, hence the overweight problem. We also determined we could have gone home and made love in the same length of time with less calories. I had not been at home at night for nearly two weeks. I wondered why we didn't.

12 midnight. Heard the frogs again, the ones Bea thought were wild pigs grunting in the drainage ditches. I am sure they were copulating; the racket was the rivals, cheering the victorious on. The nightbirds' call was not, "whip-poor-will", but "where-there's-a-will", and I added, "there's-a-way." I walked with a decision heavy on my mind: whether or not to take Dad to the large regional hospital for dialysis.

My Dad was eighty-three, total right-side paralysis with brain atrophy of 3.2 cm's wide, according to the last scan, a fractured left hip, repaired with a steel universal joint, and now – total renal failure. There had been not one drop of urinary output for the past twenty-four hours. The doctor shook his head and called in more doctors who also shook their heads.

For years I had heard Dad say, as Mom had said, "When it's my time, let me go." We, my sister and I, wrote the letter today: Dear Doc, no mechanical life support systems but all possible measures for comfort. So, who is to say when it is his time to go or what constitutes comfort? Is dialysis a mechanical life support or just a sophisticated treatment? With nearly twenty years in nursing, each moment dedicated to prolonging life for just one more day –who am I kidding? Dedicated to prolonging life until the next shift comes on duty! Isn't this "holding on," by whatever means, in conflict with the "death with dignity" philosophy to which my parents subscribed? Treatment by dialysis would be expensive. Dad's ambition, in later *years, was to leave each of his daughters "a little something". There would be little to divide if we elected to go for dialysis. Should money be a factor?*

Don't wear nylons with jogging shoes; you will surely get blisters. I thought the rain had washed the perfume of the trees away, at first, when I started walking, but then the wind changed direction and there it was, an unforgettable moment associated always with Florida. Marvelous world. My flesh crawled with pleasure in the night air. The high from a three-mile walk was second only to sex, and a fair substitute, for now.

Decision made.

When I returned from my walk, I threw the pumpkin pie in the trash can. At supper we'd had a delicious Wisconsin Cheese soup (calorie count unavailable) and for dessert, fresh, rich carrot cake with cream cheese icing —at least three or four hundred calories. Total today, well over one thousand, and I missed the bike ride.

The fear of death has taken hold. Dad wants the light on bright, he who always wanted it so dark. Now he calls, "see, see" when it is off. His respirations are moist and audible even with oxygen going. A subclavian vein drip has been reduced to a minimum, to be used for administration of medication only: he cannot hold more fluid.

The light in the room drives the moonlight away and the hospital odor is stronger than the faint orange blossoms. Will he last until morning, until the transfer can be arranged? I wonder if his heart can stand the strain; he has never heard of aerobics or cardiopulmonary fitness; his jogging shoes were mid-calf brown boots; his warm-up suit was flannel underwear under a red/black checked mackinaw.

I feel cold and lost tonight. Now it becomes clear: If – when— my father dies, I become the 'older generation' and I am not ready for that. I don't feel old. I am young, alive, and I want to stay a girl, Daddy's little girl, like I have always been. My weight gain makes me look matronly and my dieting at this time is an expression of that wish to stay young. Daddy, don't leave me. Not yet.

April 1, Day Five

8 a.m. This morning I feel terrible and roam the halls to keep awake. Dad does not seem to know when I come and go. Good note for the day: My belt is a new one, one-inch smaller hole, comfortably.

Weight loss: Still at five pounds.

Breakfast: black coffee. Reason? Nothing else available. Ray will eat at The Clock, waffles, bacon . . . Note to serious dieters: Never, NEVER skip breakfast.

10 a.m. We wait for the doctor to come. Dad in a stupor unless moved. My sister comes to talk; our decisions are identical although reached independently: We will ask for a transfer and go for dialysis. If dialysis will make him more comfortable, for whatever time he has left, it will be worth the effort, whatever the cost. Bea leaves for the office and Dad and I wait together. When Mom was dying with cancer Dad stayed with her during the day, and I stayed at night, until the last few days. Then we stayed together, waited together. Would it be that way this time? Just Dad and I?

The lab tech comes to draw blood but there are no veins left; all are obscured by the terrible edema. His hands are melon-round, the fingers touching when fully spread, the fluid can be seen beneath the surface and the skin is tight, smooth, and shiny.

The doctor is notified that the tests cannot be done and our decision to try dialysis is communicated to him. We wait for instructions.

12 Noon. My dear Aunt comes to relieve me but I cannot leave—I must see the doctor. A niece arrives and brings two small children to sit outside the window, standing in the fresh grass to hold them up to see Great Granddaddy. But Great-Granddaddy does not respond.

8 p.m. The transfer process is lengthy, wait for this doctor to call that doctor and wait again for return calls. As the hours drag on, I realize that no one has hope for recovery; if the medical and nursing staff thought it were practical, even possible, it would be given higher priority. Were they waiting, hoping the situation would resolve itself? The diarrhea and vomiting were continuous when he was awake; the comatose state has been a reprieve from the constant cleaning and changing. Bea joins me and we wait for the ambulance, arrangements finally complete. Dad rouses only briefly when moved but seems to understand our explanations.

12 Midnight. The new doctor, a Nephrologist, is young, energetic and optimistic; we feel good about making the move, regardless of the outcome. He asks about the letter, a copy of which was sent with Dad's records, and we quickly explain that we consider dialysis a treatment, for comfort, even though it is sometimes life sustaining. Just don't place him on a respirator –it is his wish—and the doctor understands our position. He begins treatment immediately, even at midnight. As the nursing staff take over, it is a relief to be treated like family.

April 2 –Day Six

3 a.m. Bea and I walk around the hospital which covers a large city block. There is no traffic. It is strangely quiet. Far down the street a policeman has pulled a car over, blue light flashing, and a young female in high heels tries to walk the crack in the sidewalk as a sobriety test. We cross the street to a newspaper rack to get the early edition as he writes out a ticket. Bea comments wonder what she did. We return to the empty lobby and read, talking little, waiting.

5a.m. The doctor gives us an encouraging report; we hurry to Dad's room and find him resting, respirations quiet and regular, edema dramatically reduced. His face is angular again, his eyes, open wide. I take his hand, his good left hand, and it seems so small; the flesh hangs loosely, wrinkled and blue, but his grip on my hand is good.
We get recognition and a faint cry of pleasure in return for our smiles and tears. We tell him to rest and watch as he goes to sleep, a normal, restful sleep, and we begin to hope for a return of renal function.

6 a.m. The hospital snack shop is clean and quiet, the coffee smells fresh and the warm Danish has silver slices of almonds in the glaze. We select the largest of the rolls and carry them to a corner table; we sit facing across the table and smile at each other, my sister, and I.

Breakfast: Danish (?) My calorie counter is in the car, but it doesn't matter. Who wants to know how many calories are in a Danish?

—⚏—

WHY I HATE NURSING

By Jane Doe, R. N.

One of our eminent Cardiologists and I stood by the side entrance to the Medical Wing discussing his probable discharges for the weekend, which I would handle for him as he would be out of town. We desperately needed beds for new admissions. The nursing station was ten feet away. A young unit secretary threw charts rapidly into a rack for another waiting physician, answered patient call lights, the telephone, and numerous questions from several nurses, both R.N.'s and L.P. N's who were milling about in the enclosed area.

A patient light kept coming on, insistently buzzing for attention. The Secretary would answer, "May I help you?" and a weak, male voice would reply, "Yes, please."

"What do you want? She would ask, and to this there was no reply. She would turn the light off and resume collecting charts for the waiting physician. The nurses at the station neither looked up nor bothered to get up.

A visitor approached the desk, an elderly woman, tall and thin, graceful, but obviously upset. "Would someone please come quickly?" She gripped the edge of the desk. "There is a terrible problem."

The unit secretary began asking questions, which room? Who was the patient? The woman, trying to answer, became confused at the many questions and began twisting her hands. None of the nurses looked up from their paperwork. They would become involved when the secretary determined which patient, looked on the assignment sheet to see who had that patient for the day, then called them to come.

Excusing myself from the heart specialist, I went to the lady, took her arm, and said, "Show me the problem."

"Thank God! Oh, thank God!" she cried. She led me down the hall, six or seven doors from the desk. The call light was blinking monotonously over the door, dinging away, unanswered. She stopped just short of the door.

"He's my brother-in-law," she said. "He would be so upset if he knew I saw him like this."

When I stepped through the door, I understood her feelings. An elderly man stood by his bed, naked, hospital gown dangling over the I.V. tubing still connected to an IVAC. Siderails were up, he had crawled over them. A straight chair was by the bed and on it sat a blue plastic bedpan, running over with liquid brown stool. The same soft, watery fluid covered his hands, the sheets, and ran down both legs, puddling in the floor. The toilet tissue sat on the overbed table on the far side of the bed. He was using a corner of the gown, trying to clean himself as I came to his side. He looked up at me, tears on his face, and said, "I've never been in such a mess in my entire life –not ever. I called and called, and nobody came."

The call bell kept dinging, and no one answered. It rang while I washed him and sat him on a clean chair. At long last a young R.N. –one of the 'pool' nurses—hired by the day, not really a member of the hospital staff—came in. She began scolding the elderly man: "I told you not to get out of bed!"

"But the paper ..." he began, but it was clear to him that she wasn't listening, so he stopped trying to explain. She took over the cleanup, no thank you to me, and I returned to the desk. The cardiologist had left, not having time to wait for me, and he left a list of discharges with the harried unit secretary to give to me.

At the end of the shift, as I signed the payroll voucher for that pool nurse, I listened to a long list of excuses, where she had been, what she was doing, without a word of thanks for my help, and, more important, not a word of concern for that poor patient. I felt half ill: one step by that poor gentle man, one move on that wet, shit-slick floor, and we would have had another hospital-related accident, a broken hip, or worse. He might not survive. I thought of all the nurses who had heard that call light, had seen that blinking light and walked on by, kept walking, because it was not their patient. I couldn't be everywhere. Like the old man, I thought, "I've never been in such a mess in my entire life."

A few days ago, the telephone rang at the surgical nursing station. The secretary answered, listened briefly, then said, "You'd best talk to the supervisor." She handed the phone to me.

After identifying myself, I listened also: "I'm sending Henry Ables over. He has maggots in the dressing on his foot. He just came *out of the hospital and he tells me the dressing wasn't changed by the blank, blank nurses. Now he's got an infection and could lose his foot due to the -blank, blank nursing care."*

When the physician stopped cursing and paused for breath, I asked, "Is your patient there with you now, Doctor?"

"Yes, He is, and he's got a rag full of maggots on his foot! I want the names of every nurse who worked on that floor! I want the Administrator notified!"

"Doctor Smith, do you realize you are placing the hospital in a position for a lawsuit as well as yourself, by talking like this in front of your patient?"

There was a short silence at his end of the line, then, in a slightly modified tone, he continued, "Henry will be there within the hour. I suggest you get ready for him."

We transferred patients around to make available a private room, since isolation was required. Henry was admitted. The R.N. team leader went to lunch. The LPN got sick and nearly fainted in the room. An older, experienced woman designated a 'nursing assistant' due to lack of a license, assisted me while we removed the bandage and washed the maggots out with Betadine. It seems Henry owns and operates a garbage pick-up and disposal service. He hadn't "gone back to work," but he "just drove the truck a couple of days to help the boys out." The accusations against the nurses had been intended to get the hospital bill paid —and it worked. I'm still waiting for Dr Smith to apologize, or even give a friendly smile. He was sent photocopies of the nursing notes which documented dressing changes and wound condition daily. Now, we can't let Doctor Smith make rounds alone; we can't depend on what he would say about the nursing staff to a patient. This creates another burden on an over-worked staff.

Our Coronary Care Director is a young nurse, brilliantly trained in one of the large teaching institutions. Her skill is such that we often consult her on technical problems rather than the physicians. Our staffing requirements are given top priority in the CCU with never less than two in the unit, even if only one patient. When the unit gets unexpectedly busy, we send help from the Medical floor until "on call" people arrive. This often leaves the floor short of help and overworked.

One evening recently we had twenty-two elderly patients to feed or assist with feeding for the evening meal, and only eight nurses available, I called our highly skilled CCU Director and asked for the extra R.N. she had. She refused, saying they were too busy. My earlier survey of the unit had not indicated this, so I decided to take a minute to walk back to the unit. As I entered the door of the Unit, I saw the R.N. "extra" go out the other door, sweater and purse in hand. She would take "on call" pay before she would go out on the floor to feed patients. Let them eat a cold meal—or not eat at all!

The following day I expressed my unhappiness over the incident to the Medical-Surgical Director. She supported the CCU Director, saying, they couldn't afford to pay a "specialty Nurse", just to feed patients! The extra R.N. had a degree—she couldn't be expected to feed patients!

Mr. and Mrs. Olsen had a silvery aura surrounding them. She was bright, shiny silver, he somewhat tarnished with a blurred, less distinct line, but then he was in bed with tubes connecting him to bottles and machines while she moved freely about the room, frequently out in the hall or to the snack bar or lobby. She wore exquisite little silk dresses, about a size three, petite, and soft-crocheted slippers, noiseless on the polished floor. Once, when I stopped by on rounds, she told me they had been married fifty-four years; she was fourteen and he was twenty. They had never been apart. She tended him meticulously, tucking, and turning, and cleaning constantly. As the illness wore on and on, she became more apprehensive, nervously watching every breath and she began calling the nursing station more frequently.

One day recently, as I worked in my office on time schedules, I gradually became aware of a lengthy conversation taking place outside my door.

"She's in the way, we can't get our work done."

"She calls constantly and for nothing!"

"Why doesn't she ever go home? She stays night and day."

"She's a nuisance, all right, "

"Let's ask the doctor for a No Visitors order. Then she can stay home, at least at night."

Curiosity got the better of me; I left my desk and asked who they were talking about. It was Mrs. Olsen. They wanted her to leave her husband of fifty years, go home alone. Then he could lie in the hospital room alone, lie there, and quietly die there, alone. Neither would pester the nurses for long.

The above unrelated but true incidents sound like the dark ages of nursing, yet all of this happened recently in a new, modern facility that is the pride of the community. But the attitude is more general than that. My father was recently hospitalized in another institution and the same feeling was discerned there. We moved across country and it is evident here as well.

On a more personal note, when I applied to hospitals in the new location, I found it necessary to go back to night duty. Twenty years of experience, most of it in supervision, meant nothing. It was "Policy that all new employees take either evening or night shift, regardless of experience or qualifications. Years of moving around due to my husband's career advancement contributed to the destruction of my career. I could "get a job" anywhere—but automatically on the night shift—this was conveyed over the phone, before an interview, before a review of my credentials, before a reference check with former employers. Yes, we want you, do you prefer 3 to 11 or 11 to 7? Any two-year graduate from a junior college could move to day shift if she had been in the same building for three years! In no other profession is years of experience *discredited so severely. My Engineer husband cannot understand: He moves upward based on ability and years in the industry. I move backwards, every time we make a change in location— yet I have remained in the same profession, accumulating more experience.*

A career change seemed to be the answer, day hours, weekends off, there is just the two of us now, our children are old enough to be left alone. A visit to the local University job placement/career planning office seemed the logical next step. A young woman, about the age of my daughter, interviewed me, and couldn't stop saying, "Twenty years in Nursing! There must be something we can salvage!"

The young advisor used a computerized search system for a list of occupations compatible with my skills and interests. The 875 occupations were quickly narrowed down to ten—ten out of 875! What a marvel of modern computer capability! All ten required a degree which would mean going back to college full time, or for nearly four years. Some credit might be given for the seventy-odd hours of University study I have completed, over and above my years of nursing, but no credit is allowed for the nursing courses. She added into the compute, "some college or technical skill required" and six jobs qualified, six out of 875.

We chose the most promising and a job description printed out automatically. Followed by: National Average Salary for this job—and it was six thousand dollars less than I made as a Nursing Supervisor.

The hard, cold facts: go back to school for four years to facilitate a career change; and then work for much less money —or stay in Nursing. My conscious mind cries don't throw it all away! Stay with the system, improve it, keep trying! My heart cries, I can't do it! I can't be everywhere, do everything, I can't stand the strain, the responsibility, the dying, the pain. I am truly, truly burned out. The conflict is agonizing.

There was another possibility: Complete a degree in Nursing, turn to education, away from direct patient care, which is where my burn-out seems to be. The seventy hours would count toward a nursing degree, even if the nursing wouldn't! the next step was to the Curriculum development office for an evaluation of my credits and the conference with the educator was encouraging. With my seventy hours above the nursing, I could take one class each quarter for the next five years and have my degree. At that time, I could afford to make a career change! A total career change, or, I possibly would have worked my way back to day shift —if my husband stayed in the same position. Only five years!

If you see a little old gray-haired grandmother in a white uniform plodding about the local campus carrying High School Algebra and Spanish I textbooks, it is probably me. Stop and say hello. Chances are, I was your night nurse the last time you were in the hospital —the one who answered your call light on the first ding.

P.S. My husband read this, and said, "I don't like the title. Why don't you call it, "Profession in Distress?" My daughter read it and said, "Why don't you use your real name?"

You work, day to day, trusting your efforts to be done for good, for life, through the hardships and unexpected inconveniences, with some good luck along the way. Always working for life, not death, and at the end, you have made the journey aiming for the plus side of the ledger, with hope and with love.

FIVE

SING

Raunchy little Blue Jay,
The force of your voice
Bends the branch whereon you sit.

Your harsh noise
Disturbs the early morn,
But the blue-on-blue

Of your bright wing
Makes my earth-torn
Heart lift —and sing.

–Betty Roberts

Lookout Platform
Virginian Railroad Bridge
Photo by Alyssa B Weisner

"Cataloochee"
Oil on Canvas by Betty Roberts

My second husband was an engineer who had been a team member under Dr. Werner Von Braun, the German Scientist who put the man on the moon. Now he worked as a defense contractor for the Army. When one contract ended, he would always find another one, sometimes requiring us to move to wherever the new job was located. We bounced from Alabama to Florida and back again three times, and once, the last move, to Georgia.

For a while, after we had been married a few years, I worked on a second book, but my husband was not supportive of my writing, always finding something else we needed to be doing. In one move, the book got boxed up with the rest of my scribbling and was put on a closet shelf.

Life moved on. I retired from nursing after our short stay in Georgia, and began classes in oil painting, a new hobby which was time consuming. Oddly, my husband enjoyed my painting. He could sit in his lounge chair, happy with the weather channel on T. V. while I spent hours painting. With my large family, I had no problem getting rid of my pictures.

It was the seventh of April, and I had just read Charles Frazier's "Cold Mountain" for the fourth time. Before reading his book, I had been thinking about (and dreaming) about a painting of the mountains where I had grown up, in southern West Virginia. The painting would show multiple mountain ranges, moving off into the blue haze, away from me in row after row. It was with exhilaration that I read his description, using strange words like scarp and crag. What is a scarp anyway? Another new word was "Cataloochee", a Cherokee word meaning waves of mountains in fading rows. Thus, began my association of my dream with the word, "Cataloochee."

"CATALOOCHEE":
THE STORY OF A PAINTING

Although Frazier describes the vision of mountains as "shades of gray", my picture was not dark or depressing. My "Cataloochee" was the blue of a sunny day with blue skies and fluffy clouds and the majestic, softly rounded mountains of my native West Virginia. "Oh, the hills, beautiful hills...."

It is my belief that the depth of my feelings about these mountains can only be appreciated by those who have experienced the actual mountains, lived and learned in their shadows, taught early to raise your head, to look up, to take life on the chin—and love it.

On March 16ᵗʰ I made a long, 700-mile trip to Florida to see two of my sisters. On this drive I was up and down the hills of southern Appalachian Mountains and could see row after row of hazy blue mountains. I came home aching to commit my dream to canvas, amateur or not, for better or worse, finally willing to try to put my vision in real form.

April 7ᵗʰ- The canvas is the largest I've ever tried, a staggering 60in. long, and 24inches wide; only such a size can begin to do justice to such a lofty aspiration. I am surprised at the amount of white oil paint required to prime it .Once the entire canvas is covered, I mix Payne's Grey in five progressively deeper shades and freehand sketch out the hills using a combination of ultramarine and Prussian Blue to paint a bright spring sky with only a few white clouds. The paint lies smooth and brushed out, and, as I prop the canvas on the mantel, I realize this is but an outline and it will be a work of many days.

A week later, lying awake for hours, I finally get up at 3: a.m., go to the den, turn on the spotlights over the mantel, and study the canvas. After breakfast I spend time with books on impressionism, painting techniques, and view mountains by Monet, Bastille, Bob

Ross, Thomas Kincaid, and my favorite, Albert Bierstadt. Now I am fearful of continuing, filled with doubts and trepidations. Who am I to attempt such a work?

More time, no progress. But I have overcome the feelings of inadequacy. Now I ask myself, "Why not? It doesn't have to be a masterpiece, just the best I can do. Why not do it for fun?" Now I realize the key is to use the impressionistic method. This will be hard to do, but worth it. I spread my books across the couch, pictures of a Bierstadt sunset, a Bob Ross tree, and best of all, Fredrick Church clouds. I can't wait until tomorrow, to try again. My pending surgery is forgotten.

Now it is May. The surgery is over, but I still cannot stand for long. I have missed a granddaughter's wedding, unable to travel. I derive much pleasure from working on the picture. It is almost like coming home to these mountains.

It is midnight. I have added foliage to the two front rows of mountains and somehow, by accident, I have achieved density, but now they are too much alike, and I have reversed my light and dark. The paint is so thick on the little trees, it will take a month to dry. Do I wait, and try a glaze to correct the color? Or—scrape it all off and try again? Scrape those thousands of little trees off? I haven't the nerve. And the clouds—hey, they 'ain't' half-bad. How I wish I had a professional to consult, like my sis in Florida, with her Master's in Art and years of teaching experience, or, like my daughter, now a teacher of art at the high school. But, overall, I am pleased, too pleased to take it all off.

I'm thinking about the foreground now, about big trees, to push the mountains back, how high should they go? I am fond of Church's "Twilight", love the trees he has done. I search through other books for examples, Good trees will make the painting; poor ones will ruin it. I must give it time to dry, so I can remove the trees if they aren't right. It is hard to stop painting and let it dry. Somehow, my picture of mountains had become a picture of clouds.

Tonight, my wish for a "pro" came true. My daughter came by, perfect timing. She gave me a couple of suggestions and agreed with what I could see needed to be done. I worked about two hours, then scraped it all off, washed it with turpentine, removing all I had done for the past two days. In spite of this, my youngest daughter came by, looked at the painting and said, "My brother and sisters can have Grandmother's paintings –I want this one."

Restless nights, awake several times with right hip pain, and when I got up, I discovered a rash above my waist, going around to my back. I knew immediately what it was, having seen it when in nursing. I had shingles. In spite of the pain, I couldn't resist working on the painting. My husband brought my easel in to my easy chair and adjusted it so I could paint sitting down. We went to Sonny's for bar-be-que, so I didn't have to cook.

The time passes so swiftly. Memorial Day weekend passed so quietly I hardly knew it was a holiday. Shingles pain has my painting put on hold, yet I think about it constantly and that somehow makes the pain better.

It is June. I feel mistreated—what did I do to deserve this pain? Today all I've accomplished is to work on the sky. The clouds are smaller now, more distant, and the colors are good, blending with the mountains, a touch of sunlight. I like it now, will let it dry and look at it again tomorrow. It may be time to start the trees and that scares me. What if I ruin it?

June fifth. Last night I slept straight through, not up for pain meds, first time in weeks. I felt like painting again, and my husband helps me hang up the laundry so I can go to my picture. It needs work on the river—or lake—I really haven't decided which it is, just "water" right now.

Back to the doctor. The medication is giving me blurred vision and the pain is severe again. Medication changed, this time to be taken for 4 weeks. My mind focuses on the painting. My pine trees are like those on the Rocky Mountains, not the eastern mountains *at all. Wiped off, started over, this time with eastern evergreens and hardwoods. But my trees look too dark, too false in their shape, no beauty of their own, neither fish nor fowl—neither cedar nor pine. I wash them all away, what isn't dry, and use sandpaper to remove the others. I cannot let the trees take away my waves of blue mountains. My "Cataloochee" would be gone.*

As soon as my husband left to go swimming, I got my "pre-mixed" paints out of the freezer and started repairing the damage I'd done the day before. I painted from each end, meeting the good part which had been left untouched. My goal was to return the picture of the mountains to where it had been before all the experimenting with large trees in the foreground. I worked steadily for three hours, then put the canvas back over the fireplace and stepped back to view it, flood lights on above it.

It was all I could do to not sit down and cry—cry with relief. I had done it! You couldn't tell where the old part began, and the new mountains ended. Now, to just let it alone, and let it dry—again. Then, some work on the water, a little on the sky, and I'll be ready to try the trees again.

Away from the painting, I think about it constantly: trees or no trees? I don't want to ruin it. Whatever I use it must be light and airy, but all my examples of trees look dark and heavy, too much foliage, or the wrong season, I stay with my grandchildren so my daughter can work, and am away from the painting through the day. At home again, I enjoy what is finished. It will be pleasing if I don't ruin it with the wrong kind of trees. We take Mom's picture of a West Virginia snow out of the frame and put my mountain scene in the gold frame.

It is amazing how much better it looks when framed. My husband says, leave it alone, you are not a painter of trees, don't mess up the mountains.

June 15th. I paint the trees. Now it looks messy—any four-year-old could have done better. The quality was gone. The only thing I was pleased with was the sky. I may be sanding down the mountains, removing the trees, replacing the mist.

What agony I am in tonight. What with the shingles pain and the pain of disappointment I don't know which is worse. It will have to dry before doing anything. It doesn't bear close inspection. There is no glow.

This a.m. I repainted the lake, putting in the clouds, the waterline, and redid areas of the mountains where they had become blurred in the many washings with turpentine. We went to my daughter's for supper and I sat on her patio and studied the way her pine trees were outlined against the sky, so graceful, so beautiful. The next morning, I took a deep breath, mixed some dark grey, white, a bit of Van Dyke brown, and drew in, from memory, the branches of my trees. No leaves yet just the trunks and larger branches. Now, let dry, again, before adding leaves. It is 81 degrees, I put the painting on the porch, turned the fans on; it will be dry by morning. My goal is to have it finished before my "out-of-town" daughter gets here on the thirtieth.

Just hope I haven't taken away from my rows and rows of mountains, with the trees. Pine trees are generally connected with immortality—their evergreen nature, but also with wildness and height, the sublime. The group of birch on the right are included for their picturesque bark, their fresh greenness, the light airy leaves, and because they are growing in the water. Like Church, I have tried to "elevate the commonplace". Whether I've succeeded at all remains to be determined. I have deliberately painted it without an inkling of "man"—it is to be as we first found it—unspoiled by humans. I almost hate to finish it.

We eat supper at Greenbrier and when we get back, I look at what I had painted. Part of it looked okay, but I took an old t-shirt, soaked it in turpentine and washed off most of what I had painted this morning. My husband tells me to leave it alone, that I am trying to create the perfect picture and that can't be done. He seems to like it as it is, and so do I, but yet – I hate to think it is finished. I don't want it to end.

We took my "Cataloochee" to Frame world to have it framed. When we got home the mantle looked extremely bare and I felt the absence of the painting deeply.

On Tuesday morning I woke up, the picture clear in my mind. The birch trees could stay, the mountains, the sky, the water, was all okay. But the pine trees had to go. We picked up the picture, and it was not until we had it once again on the mantle that I realized the frame we had purchased was exactly like the one on Mom's snow picture. I study my pine trees—they could be left if I took off the lower branches, lightened the needles – no. The pine trees had to go. If I took them off, it would mess up the mountains. Could I repaint the mountains? I hadn't saved the paint, would have to start from scratch to mix it. I can do better, I told myself. I have to try.

My daughter has come and gone. The kids, all together, had given me a surprise birthday dinner, and I was pleased, but very surprised. We had played Canasta all evening. My painting was a success, in that everyone said they loved it.

We have hung the "Cataloochie" over the fireplace in the den, and it exactly fits the space. A year from now, I'll take it down, clean it, and varnish it. I'm pretty sure it will live on, maybe more than one generation.

Two short years after he retired my husband began showing signs of Alzheimer's. The disease soon put an end to our traveling, and we were practically confined to our home as his illness increased in severity. Almost immediately, I returned to my writing, keeping a journal as he progressed from early Stage One, to the final Stage Seven, a period of almost ten years. As wife, nurse, and caregiver, my second book, "Midnight Chronicles," became my second published work. Again, my writing became an outlet for all the pain and sorrow.

Through the years, our children made every effort to give their love and support to both of us, but the greater burden fell to our youngest daughter who moved from out of state, relocating to be nearby when we needed her. She had been so young when we married, he was truly a father to her. She was my strong support when I began putting my journal notes on the computer and organizing them for publication. We completed the book and sent it off for publication while he was in the Veterans Nursing Facility where he spent his last year. I ended the book without addressing his last days.

MIDNIGHT CHRONICLES:

A Love Story
(excerpt, book published in 2018)

"I'm sorry, honey, I just woke up and started remembering and regretting and —Oh, God!" Paul burst into hard sobs, his shoulders shaking. He kept turning his head side to side on the pillow. "There's nothing you can do. It's not your fault. . . it's just, oh, God! I am so lonesome! I feel like I am somewhere out in space all by myself, all alone!"

Again, I tried to reassure him, telling him he was not alone, that I was there, but he didn't seem to hear me or even know me. This went on for over ten minutes, but finally he sat up and swung his feet to the floor. "It's not your fault, honey," he said over and over. "I just feel so alone."

I didn't try to console him again. I just lay beside him, waiting to see if he wanted to talk. In the stillness after the storm, I realized I was not the woman he was "remembering and regretting." He was locked into the past. His divorce had been painful for him, instigated by his first wife. It had been very difficult for his two children as well. Paul had been climbing the corporate ladder, working long hours, traveling frequently as required, and the marriage had fallen apart. Now, along with his constant memories of the National Guard, he was reliving those difficult times, times when he, apparently, had been alone indeed.

A few nights ago, I was sitting in my lounge chair in the den, reading. Paul had been to bed and to sleep for a couple of hours. I heard him stir, and in a moment his bedside light came on. "What are you doing?" he called.

"Reading," I replied. "Do you need something?"

"Could you talk to me? I've got a question."

It was already one o'clock in the morning. I was only a few pages from the end of my book and had planned to go to bed as soon as I finished it. I put the book down, went to the bedroom and sat down in the chair by his bed.

"Honey, I don't remember having sex."

Dumfounded, I looked at him. Was he conning me? Was he serious? I didn't know how to answer him. Finally, I blurted out, "Are you serious?"

"Yes, dead serious," he said. "I've been lying here, trying to figure out how we would do it. We've both gotten so large."

"Hey now! I'm not that big!" I laughed, trying to lighten the mood.

He was so somber, so worried looking. How do I handle this? I have very little interest in sex now, because over the past few years it seemed like I ended up with a problem, either raw, or scratched, and my skin was so fragile now. A few years ago, Paul had received microwave treatments for enlarged prostate and that had seemed to affect his ability. For the past few years, we had limited our activities to kisses and hugs. He seemed so serious now; this wasn't a time to take him lightly.

"Honey, I'm sorry. We've had a very good sex life for many years. I don't think it's something I miss now. I'm happy the way we are."

"Well, I'd like to have sex once in a while, if you could handle it, but I don't want to force you, or cause you problems, and I don't want to neglect you if there's something I'm supposed to be doing —but I can't remember what I'm supposed to do . . . "

"Please don't be concerned, honey," I said as I slipped into bed beside him. "We're just fine, just like we are. If there's something I need, I'll let you know, and you do the same. We'll be just fine." He put his arms around me, holding me close.

I thought of the many memories I had, particularly from the years after we were first married. The fact that he had lost those years saddened me deeply, but I couldn't cry now, not in front of him; he would feel like he wasn't a good husband. Those times were over now, and he had retreated to his younger years, so the desire was there. I knew he was dwelling on sex because of his descriptions of his hallucinations.

I couldn't help but think back to some of the elderly patients I'd had in the nursing facilities. It hadn't been unusual for some of them to try to look down the front of their caregiver's uniform or put a hand up their skirt. And, yes, they had known what they were doing. My next thought was, if we were intimate, would he know who I was? A couple of nights ago, when I came to bed, he had reached over and patted me on the fanny.

"Who are you?" he'd said.

My answer was almost (note I said almost) "I'm the milkmaid!" Instead, I replied, "I'm your best buddy."

Now, how do I handle this aspect of my husband's illness? His arms were tight around me, and he started talking, telling me again how much he loved me, and that I was the best thing that had happened to him, just as he had been saying nightly for the past few months. Suddenly he switched subjects, telling me how lonely he was, saying again he felt he was out in space, nobody there, looking for someone to bring him in, to stop the floating. Again, I didn't know what to say, except to repeat what I always said, "I'm here, honey, I'm here." All this time I had been lying with my head on his shoulder. He began to move and I realized I was lying on the shoulder that pained him so much. I moved off but continued to snuggle close beside him. Gradually, his conversation drifted, and he began his usual nighttime questions: "How many kids do we have? Where are they? Do they come to see us?" His questions slowed, and finally I heard his soft snore; he was asleep.

Quietly, I slipped out of bed. Sleep for me was impossible. I went back to the den, but instead of my book, I pulled a small paperback from my bookcase, a book that I'd read frequently over the years, a book about the meaning of life written by a man who almost lost his. Viktor Frankel had addressed sex and love; it was easy to find his comments, and I read them again.

"Normally, sex is a mode of expression of love," he wrote. "Sex is justified, even sanctified, as soon as, but only as long as, it is a vehicle of love. Thus, love is not understood as a mere side effect of sex but sex as a way of expressing the experience of that ultimate togetherness that is called love."

Paul, in his aloneness due to Alzheimer's was searching for a way to achieve that togetherness, a way to relieve that terrible feeling of isolation, of being lost. The tears ran down my cheeks as I put the book away. I had failed him when he needed me most. In spite of all my caring, all my awareness of what he was going through, I had failed him.

My routine had been, do what had to be done, then get in the car and drive to the nursing home, sit with him, even when he didn't know I was there, then come home. My husband died in January, after developing swallowing problems, and then pneumonia.

For the first time in my life, I was living alone, and somewhat at a loss as to what to do with my days. My smart daughter said, "All right, Mom. It's time to get "our" book out and finish it." Our book, as she called it, was the one I had started so long ago. She had taken the first part of it to her English teacher to read/ correct, and she hadn't forgotten it. She was in high school then, and I hadn't unboxed the book since.

It was March, and even though we live in the south, it was cold, rainy, and often too unpleasant to get outside. I began a frenzied cleaning spree, dragging out boxes long abandoned on closet shelves, giving away the closet full of dress shirts and khaki pants, and shoes, jackets, ties. My husband had been a tall man, but we had tall sons and sons-in-law, and grandsons ...it didn't take long.

I was left with boxes of paperwork, including the long-neglected book. It had been waiting for me, and I grabbed it like an abandoned child grabs a friendly hand.

Last week, "our book", once titled "The Mountaineers", now renamed, "In the Shadow of The Bridge," went to the printers. My third book, a coming-of-age historical novel, set in the mountains of West Virginia, has been a "coming home" experience for me, a reuniting with my childhood, and with my early family. It has been totally absorbing, delightfully occupying my days –and many nights—until we felt we had done the best we could, and it was time to let it go, let it face the world on its own merits, and a future yet unknown. My hope is, it will have something to travel on, its own truth, its own lasting memory.

IN THE SHADOW OF THE BRIDGE

(excerpt from book published March 2020)

She lay dreamily in the thick grass, her head shaded by the blooming day Lilies against the side of the house. Last summer, on a Sunday afternoon, the porch had been full of laughing youths, Will and Ben, Mary Beth, Hollie and Emmett, Shirley with Bun. Now only Jane and Ted sat there. Will, Ben, and Emmett were gone, Shirley was dead, Hollie and Mary Beth stayed home, each alone. The camp was so still the rasping of grasshoppers seemed an intrusion.

She sat up and reached for the Sunday paper. Dagwood and Blondie had named their baby daughter, "Cookie", no note about who had won the contest. Well, that's as good as "Bun", she thought. The word 'bomber' caught her eye and sitting cross-legged in the grass, she started reading: Called a B-19, World's largest airplane, cost over three million dollars, a wing-spread of two hundred and twelve feet—why, that was as long as —as— she couldn't visualize what two hundred looked like. A hundred and thirty feet long, forty-two feet high. How high was her house? Mother had wall-papered the living room; she remembered the ceiling was twelve feet high, two stories, twenty-four feet –this plane was twice as high as her house! She folded the paper and kept it handy for Edgar, hoping he would come over.

Top speed of two hundred and ten miles per hour. Fantastic! Range, over seven thousand miles –nearly twice as far as Lindbergh had flown. Crew of ten—Edgar as pilot, she'd be co-pilot, Joe could be navigator, if he'd play right without clowning, BillynBob, Bun, Judith if Mrs. Gillespie would let her come out, still room for three more passengers'! What a plane! Her eyes lifted to the sky, imagining the plane flying higher than the mountain tops – and she saw a break in the clouds: the sun was glinting behind them, leaving bright, white edges. A cloud with a silver lining, a good omen, but, at the moment, the only ones sharing her vision were Jane and Ted McKinney.

Sometime later Edgar threw himself down beside her on the cool grass. They lay on their backs, studying the clouds, deciding if they wanted to fly over them or under them; the silver-lined ones were gone. She told Edgar about the B-19, and he read the article. "Land at sixty miles an hour—faster than we drive a car," said Edgar, whistling. "Takes eleven thousand gallons of gasoline. No wonder we're going to be rationed soon!"

"Think it will come to that?"

"Sure, and before long, too. Pa says before winter."

"How come your Pa never talks?"

"Why, he does talk!" said Edgar, surprised.

"Not to me, not to anybody 'cept you and Joe."

"Well, he's not the talking kind."

"Where did your mother go, Edgar? What really happened?"

Edgar was quiet for a bit, rolled over on his stomach, and put the grass blade between his thumbs, making a whistle. "Tell you sometime," he said, and blew a long, raucous sound.

"Hey! You'll wake Mother and Daddy!"

Obediently, Edgar dropped the grass blade. He nodded toward the railroad bridge. "Be hot up there, but at least there'd be a breeze."

"I'm going up there someday, "said El.

"Been there."

"On the bridge?"

"Yep."

"When?"

"Oh, lots of times. Mostly at night. Can't nobody see you if you're keerful."

"It's against the law.

"Naw, no harm."

"I've seen the signs: unlawful to trespass, railroad property."

"What they don't know won't hurt them."

"You could get hurt."

"Naw, not if you know how."

"Take me."

"What?"

"Take me up on the bridge—I've wanted to go for years and years and years!"

Edgar was silent, thoughtful. Then, "All right, but you've got to do exactly what I tell you."

"Oh, I will! Honest, I will."

"Promise?"

"Promise, cross my heart and hope to die!"

Edgar laughed. "That's exactly what you might do if you don't watch out! Okay, tonight, after everyone's asleep. You watch for me; I'll give the signal. We've got to wait until after the 9:30 freight comes, then there's plenty of time before the next one comes along. Got to know the schedule, that's real important, can't get caught up there by surprise, got to plan it."

El was so excited she could hardly eat supper. By eight-thirty she had Bun in the tub and had read several stories. Bun finally went to sleep. She listened to Mother and Daddy getting ready for bed, watched for Jane's light to go out. She exchanged her nightgown for shorts and shirt, put on her winter shoes and laced them tightly as Edgar had instructed, so she could run over the crossties or gravel, depending on the situation. Edgar said Mr. Reeves made his last round 'bout nine - thirty, and after that, they were on their own: not a soul to stop them.

The moon, rising late now in the last half of its cycle, cast a faint glow on the bridge, but in the shadows, low in the valley, it was as black as a mine hole without a lamp. The 9:30 freight rumbled by overhead, each car bumping over one loose rail on the westbound track, de-bump, de-bump, de-bump and a few *empties added their lighter clack-clack-clack-clackity-clack. Soon it was gone, its lonesome-sounding whistle blowing long and uninterrupted, the signal for approaching a crossing or a station. By the time the red caboose had passed over the bridge, the engine, an EL-3A, specially built by General Electric for the Virginian, would be almost to the passenger station at Herndon. As the sound faded down the valley, El saw Edgar standing in the road. She slipped the screen off the window, crawled down the porch roof, caught the post with her feet, slid down to the porch rail, and dropped lightly on the thick sod of her yard. She waited for Edgar to lead, followed him across the triangle and into the deeper shadows of the bridge.*

Her heart was racing audibly; not only was she sneaking out at night with a boy—a sin worse than death—but she was going on the railroad bridge, the one area of the camp which was strictly, absolutely forbidden. Off-limits, even to adults.

What if Mother checked her room? What if Bun woke up, what if—but soon her worries were forgotten. They crossed the footbridge over the creek, slipped by the haunted house, and began to climb straight up the mountain, in the dark, beneath giant hardwood trees and ancient hemlocks, through heavily tangled new-blooming pink and red rhododendron bushes: she couldn't turn back now.

The woods were dark and quiet. She stepped on a pinecone and the crunch seemed louder than a firecracker. It was noticeably cooler under the trees, and gradually her eyes adjusted to the shadows; she began to see the tree trunks, to distinguish the heavier shrubs. She reached out for Edgar and found he was reaching for her; their hands met and she felt secure. An owl hooted over the rise and El jumped. She thought about the bobcat that had frightened Jane and wished she hadn't remembered it.

"Are there bobcats in these woods?" she whispered to Edgar.

"Sure, I guess so, "he answered. "You don't have to whisper; nobody can hear us now."

El thought it disrespectful, like talking in church or something. Although unable to express it, she felt solemnity was needed to validate the occasion. The deep night stillness isolated them from the town, from all people; they were alone now in a new, unexplored, primordial world, dependent upon each other for survival. She felt very close to Edgar in a new and exciting way; whatever happened, they were in it together.

His hand guided her up the steep slope with a surety born of familiarity, and in a few minutes, breathing hard, they reached the railroad tracks. Edgar leaned over from the waist, his hands on his knees, regaining his breath, and El slowed hers in the usual way, breathing through her nose, one-Mississippi, two-Mississippi

"Now we can talk," said Edgar, "and you won't have to worry about bobcats much longer —they won't come out on the bridge—got too much sense."

"Why did we come out on the tracks so far from the bridge?"

"Too steep. Too hard to climb right at the bridge".

Edgar was walking the crossties easily, shortening his steps to hit each one. El could see the steel rail, shining faintly in the near-moonlight, and chose to walk it, beside him rather than behind. As they walked, he instructed.

"Now, if you get dizzy, just sit down. Don't try to walk on the bridge dizzy, that'd be dumb. And if a train ever catches you on the bridge, lay down, don't run, and whatever you do, keep your head. Lay down between the tracks," he demonstrated by dropping face down on the heavy wooden sleepers.

"Lay on your hands so they don't get chopped off."

El shuddered at the thought of losing her fingers; she could see herself going home with her fingers missing, red blood dripping. "You're sure the train can go over you?"

"Yep," said Edgar, springing to his feet.

"Ever tried it?"

"Nope, and I don't intend to! All it takes is clocking the schedule, and keepin' your ears washed out."

They reached the end of the bridge. El was struck by the size of it! It was so much larger than it looked from below; the tracks were wider, and there was space between them, plenty of room for her to fall through. From the road below, it had looked like a tiny crack between the two tracks. From below, the catenary poles looked like short posts. Now, standing beside them, she could see they were as tall as the electricity poles in her front yard.

"I can't see the other end," she whispered.

"Of course not. There's a curve in it, and it's got seventeen spans!"

"I'm scared," whispered El.

Protective at once, Edgar reached for her hand. "Don't be—it's great once you get out in the middle. Come on, I'll hold you."

She tightened her grip on his hand and started out on the rail but Edgar stopped her. "No, it's best to walk on the ties, and set your foot down flat cause if it goes between, you'll stumble and might go through, or pitch over."

El shuddered at the thought of pitching over the side. Carefully they worked their way to the middle of the bridge, moving a few steps, pausing to let El look around. When she was moving, she refused to look anywhere except where her next step was to be. At the center of the bridge, Edgar stopped her.

"Careful now, step over the rail. We are at the lookout."

She did as he instructed and gained the small wooden platform projected outward from the tracks on the side next to the schoolhouse and the company store. She took a deep breath and looked about. It was like being on top of the world! She could see the thin edge of the moon just topping the trees, its light not yet reaching the valley below. The stars were much closer now, clearer without the mountains overpowering them. She gradually became aware of a faint hum, a constant musical but monotonous tone, *and turned to Edgar. "What's that?" she whispered. "Wind in the wires," he said aloud. She looked again at the tall catenary poles and thought of her father, climbing those poles all year long, in every kind of weather, climbing them on top of all the bridges on the Virginian railroad system. She felt exhilarated, thrilled at being up so high, and realized that her Daddy probably felt the same way, or he wouldn't do it. She looked below and expected to feel dizzy but found that the amazing height didn't bother her at all. She could see the roof of the schoolhouse –there was a cap, a red cap, lying on the other side. And she could see the roof of the company store; the two-story structure looked so big when she was on the ground, but now it looked no larger than her house.*

She could see the creek winding around behind the company store, behind the haunted house, disappearing as the bridge blocked her view. She turned, indicating she wanted to see the other side, see the creek, the road, her house, all of it. Edgar held her arm as she crossed over to the other side and looked down.

Seeing her house was a shock; how small it looked, yet how clearly she could see every detail, including the white lace curtain hanging out of her window, blowing on the roof of the front porch—a certain give-away. Next time, she would take the time to replace the window screen.

They sat straddling the crossties, their feet through the spaces between and dangling below the bridge as they inspected the town. The air moved about them, cooler now, sweet-scented and free. There was a light in one of the houses near the end of the camp by the highway, and Edgar, pointing, said, "Mrs. Margaret's. She never left it on afore he died, but now it burns every night, leastways every weekend. It must be near ten o'clock. Watch now."

"Watch what?" she whispered.

"You'll see," he said, and added, "You don't have to whisper, can't be heard this fer up."

They sat in silence for a while, but as the moon slowly cleared the trees the beauty of the scene overcame her. She stood up, moved to the small look-out platform and threw her arms wide, spreading them as if she would fly, like a bird spreads its wings. Love for the hills, for the dark, silent trees, for the light of the moon with its reflected sun-glory shining on her face, love for her world, its symmetry and congruency, its fluid loveliness, washed over her in orgasmic waves and she felt a part of it all.

"Oh, Edgar! I wish I could fly!"

Edgar answered with male practicality. "Someday, I'm going to, just as soon as I get old enough." He spread his arms for wings and made the sweeping motions of a plane diving and swooping, walking the rail as gracefully as a mountain cat. "I'll have me one of those dive bombers!"

That was not the kind of flying El meant but she couldn't explain her depth of emotion.

Edgar stopped suddenly, reached for her and pulled her down to lie flat on the tracks. "Shush!"

Staying low he moved to the camp side of the tracks, motioning for her to follow. "Stay down," he whispered. "Look"

Coming down the road from Mrs. Margaret's house was Mr. Collins, striding along briskly but quietly, hands in his pockets. He turned off the road beside the Gillespie house and walked on the concrete wall bordering the creek to his back gate, disappearing beneath the great willow tree. El sat silent for a time, then asked, "Every night?"

"Nah, every weekend. Pa says he's too old for every night."

"You told your Pa?"

"Didn't hafta. He seen 'em too."

"Your Pa was up here?"

"Yep."

"With you?"

"Yep, first time. I told him I was coming, he said he'd come with me if'n I was bound to."

El tried to imagine telling her Mother or Daddy that she was going to do something that was clearly forbidden and against the law, and having them give permission, much less come with her. She gave up. It would never happen. Edgar was saying, "went hunting with me, first time, too and fishin". Like it amounted to the same thing, but El was back to Mr. Collins and Mrs. Margaret.

"And they've been seeing each other ever since he died?"

"Nah, long before that, way last fall, first time I was up here, I saw them."

She thought about all the times she had seen them out in the hall. Their smoking breaks at school. Just looking at them she should have known. Not that they ever did anything, it was more a matter of how they looked, a reaching out, or something deeper. She tried to feel romantic about it, but she just couldn't. She liked—almost loved—Mr. Collins, but she truly despised Mrs. Margaret! Mrs. Margaret didn't fit her idea of a heroine, even if she was a new widow.

Edgar reached for her hand. "We'd best be getting back," he said and led the way off the bridge, carefully, watching El's feet to be sure she was hitting the crossties squarely in the center. They slipped down the mountainside through the woods, and ran lightly to her front gate, where Edgar held it firm to prevent the squeak of the hinges and walked her to her front porch.

"Next time," he whispered, "next time we'll go all the way across!" He bent his head quickly and touched her lips with his, whispered, "night!" and ran across the road to disappear into the shadows of his own front porch.

El couldn't decide if he had really kissed her or just thought about it, it was so quick. With a tiny, happy smile she climbed to the porch roof and through her window. Wouldn't be any harm, teaching Edgar how to kiss, couldn't be anything wrong with that, *now that she knew all about babies and everything. Next time, she said to herself as she curled up beside the sleeping Bun, next time Edgar Mitchell, just wait. You just wait and see!*

(About four months later, In the Shadow of the Bridge, continued.)

El sat in her room and waited for Edgar's signal; when he came, she removed her mouse- ears cap and tail, left the red vest of her Mickey-Mouse costume behind. She slid down the porch roof dressed all in black, and pants, just as she had planned, looking just like one of the boys. As they ran to the storage house, Edgar whispered, "We're going to knock over Ol' Reeves still, but I didn't tell them it was your idea." El didn't care who got the credit, as long as she could go with them!

There were about ten of them in the group and the leader was a high school boy by the name of Jock who had been one of Ben's best friends. El knew him, but not well, because Jane didn't like him and never asked him to their house. Quietly, close together, they crept down the road to the old storage house, their shoes making a slight crunching on the cindered road, like cracking walnuts under your heel. Mr. Reeves was nowhere in sight, because, Edgar explained, Jock and his friends had led him a wild goose chase down through the camp, and them sneaked back. They'd have to be quick, Ol' Reeves wouldn't be gone long! Jock and Edgar, as the oldest, slipped up to the front door. It was locked; it wouldn't budge. Next, they tried raising a window, but it was nailed shut. "Break a window!" someone said. "No, he'd hear us!" "That's agin the law!" said another.

It was never clear, later, just who's idea it was, but it didn't matter. Once the idea was expressed, it was clear that it had been in every one's mind: they could turn over his outhouse!

With one accord, they moved to the fenced yard, trod over the cut corn stalks, through the wild sweet potato vines and saw briars, *and took their stance at the front and back of the wooden two-holer, Jock, as commander-in-chief, counted, one, two, three, and the toilet tilted, wobbled, and fell on its side. Not a kid stepped into the pit.*

As the outhouse crashed down, they let out a wild Indian cheer—who cares if Mr. Reeves hears them now! They moved as one, streaked up the back road toward the railroad—their first tactical error. Mr. Reeves, right behind them, ran just as fast, waving his arms, with the shotgun held over his head in one hand, yelling, "Hyer, Hyer! Outa here, you dang-nabbed sons of cock-fighters, you bamboozling thieves, sons of Satan's daughters, you wicked, swoogle-eyed horse-thriving' bandits, you—you –" Mr. Reeves stopped shouting, saving his breath, as he got closer and closer to the group. Some of the younger ones began dropping out, one at a time, rolling down the side of the hill, falling like green walnuts, one after the other, until only the larger boys and El were left. Jock, still in the lead shouted, "Quick! The bridge! He won't get us there!"

"Jock! No! It's time for the train!" shouted Edgar, knowing the schedule to the minute, but it was too late. Jock led his troops out on the bridge, running with practiced steps in short, jerky motions, hitting each crosstie squarely in the center. The others kept pace as best they could, and they gained the small wooden platform in the center of the bridge just as the nine-thirty freight came roaring down the mountain on the westbound track, coming square between them and Mr. Reeves who was left standing at the end of the bridge.

El stood on the very edge of the wooden perch, Edgar's arms wrapped tight around her, the wind from the fast-moving train whipping her hair into her eyes, along with cinders from the empty coal cars interspersed between the box cars of freight. The engine, an EL3A, was made up of three sections, three single units connected to increase power, and had a speed of thirty-eight miles per hour; combined as they were, and rolling down the incredible grade, the speed of the "square-heads" was closer to fifty miles per hour. The electric engines regenerate their power on the downhill stretches and the engineer, old "Long-Haul Taylor" himself, said, the faster the run, the more the power, so let'er rip, boys, let'er rip! Run'er wide open!"

The iron bridge vibrated with the thunder, swayed in the wind from the four- hundred- thousand pound monster engines; the heavy-duty rails trembled with the fierce rush of cars, whined and cried with the flat gondolas, and when the motors had passed, its whistle moaning loud and long as it blew for the Herndon crossing, the kids on the half-way deck were trembling and moaning as well: few, if any, had been on the bridge when a train went by.

They huddled together as the long train passed, not daring to move until the sound was gone, recalling the many stories they'd heard of men stepping out, thinking the way was clear, only to be hit by a second train coming behind the first.

The bridge settled again, and the boys pulled their bravado about their shoulders, shook themselves and straightened a bit taller. Old Man Reeves was forgotten with the coming of the train, and they assumed he had forgotten them also, until one of the younger boys, not as occupied with screwing up his courage, spotted the "mean man" of the town. Mr. Reeves was walking out on the bridge, walking slowly, deliberately, inexorably, the shotgun braced over his arm. From somewhere above they became conscious of a low, mournful sound, beginning softly, increasing to a loud, vibrating pitch, a ghostly wail—

Granny Hall! It was Granny Hall—making her regular Halloween night visit to the bridge!

For a fleeting instant, the group faced their new foe disconcerted, then Edgar took charge.

"Quick! This way!" he shouted, and began running to the end of the bridge, running to the steep side of the mountain, running, running, hitting the sleepers awkwardly, stumbling, pulling El *by the hand. Clawing their way across the bridge, with a new and terrible monster after them, El and Edgar ran like there was a combination of evils pursuing them, their breath caught in their throats, their mouth dry, their screams drowning out the wailing ghost and the cursing of Mr. Reeves. Finally, they tumbled headlong off the bridge into the laurel and rhododendron bushes, disappearing into the dark dead green of the night-forest inhabited only by friendly, known ghosts, gentler, familiar spooks, softer hooting owls. Once on level ground, the group dispersed rapidly, each seeking the comfort and security of their own home.*

El shimmed up the post and crept through her window without a thought to who might see her; all she wanted to do was get out of her mouse suit and into her own warm bed. She was shaking from head to toe, a combination of cold and excitement. If she had asked, Daddy would have said the ghost was electricity generated by the wide-open running of the nine-thirty fright, returning along the high wire, running up the mountain to Clark's Gap substation. But El knew better; she knew a ghost when she heard one! Frightened by Granny Hall, scared to death of Mr. Reeves —the excitement far outweighed the fear. She had satisfied one of her most secret, most cherished, life-long ambitions: she had been on the bridge when a train went by!

Betty P Roberts
Daughter, Sister, Wife, Mother, Grandmother, Great-
Grandmother, Aunt, Friend,
Registered Nurse and Author

The Virginian Railroad Caboose
Princeton Railroad Museum
Princeton, West Virginia
Betty Roberts with granddaughter Alyssa Weisner

THE LAST PAGE

It wasn't an ordinary little black book. Nevertheless, he had termed it so, as had his father: the little black book. It was small, breast-pocket size, and dark—smooth, old-brown leather, hand-stitched binding, fine-grained flax paper edged in gold. It fit comfortably in a large man's hand, fit well into the inner pocket of his suit coat. There were female names in the little black book, but not in the usual alphabetical order, Betsy, Charlotte, or Jane, notations appropriately following —naughty or nice, married or available. The names, of both genders, were inscribed in chronological order, and some were repeated more often than others: Mary Elizabeth, a frequent one, and, of course, Phillip and Scott.

The finely written entries began in the early nineteenth century, continued until the present: Mary Elizabeth Weston m. Thomas Blake Scott, 3 Aug. 1801. Mary Elizabeth Scott, b. Sept. 10, 1802. On the next page, in somewhat different handwriting but with the same pale violet ink, was scrawled, Mary Elizabeth Scott m. Phillip Howard Johnson, Dec. the Twenty-Fourth, 1823. Then, one space down, Phillip Scott Johnson, b. twentieth of January 1825. Mary Elizabeth Scott Johnson dead on this First day of the New Year, 1826. May God preserve her soul and comfort my Son in his sorrow. Page three began a careful listing of succeeding generations.

Although the recorded births, marriages, and deaths of his ancestors were meaningful to Phillip Scott Johnson, on this cold February morning they were of minor interest. He held the small book in one thin, vein-lined hand, the other grasping the plastic rod to control the venetian blind. He directed the pale morning light onto the book's pages reflecting faintly on the pale violet tracings of the early years, faded now with time, but bringing out more recent entries written in darker, more permanent ink. He skimmed over the births and deaths, concentrating instead on the pages between, pages containing the military history of the men in his family.

COL Phillip Blake Scott, though getting on in years, had served McClellan well at the battle of Antietam, Sept. 1862, dying from his wounds, proud and sharp-spoken to the end. Above his obituary line, in his own hand, were the words:

Charlemagne. Bay Mare, 7 yr. Old,
Killed under me in battle. The Union Will Be.

Thus, began the recordings of world significance. Phillip's son, though a soldier, was more scholarly, and sat behind his Washington desk all the years between the Battle of the Little Bighorn and the wretched Battle of Wounded Knee. Fourteen long years spent recording Indian attacks, but the single entry beneath his name was Transcontinental Railroad, May 10, 1869.

Phil studied the entry made in his grandfather's spidery scrawl, the same distinctive style as in numerous bound essays on Indian Affairs he had so treasured, only recently placing them in the archives of the University of Utah, a 'tip of the hat' to the era in which his grandfather had lived, an ironic recognition of the fact that his grandfather, too, had been a soldier.

He turned the page slowly, raised his head and looked unseeingly out the window. Only faint rays of light reached his solitary room, cold early light illuminating his narrow face and sunken eyes. He recalled his grandfather, smiled faintly as he read the entries. At the age of four he had been present, sitting upon his father's knee, when his grandfather had made his last entry, and he heard again the elderly voice: "This record, Phillip, originated over one hundred years ago. It is your heritage, and when I die it is your obligation to continue it. But remember, Phillip," –Grandfather had raised up in the four-poster, long white beard on his chest, and he had raised his voice, frightening the young child – "remember! Record events sparingly, my Son – most become insignificant with time!"

Phil studied the view from his window, bringing himself back to the necessity at hand. The digital watch in his ring gave the time as six-fifty. Only a few more minutes and he must leave. He could see the faint spire of the Washington monument in the hazy distance, its edges blurred by the morning mist. By leaning against the cold aluminum frame, he could see the white dome of the Capitol. He turned the pages of the little black book, handling them gently and with respect, finding his father's birth date, and beneath it the words, Served in the World War. His father, he knew, had been one of the Doughboy's wearing Boy Scout caps stationed in Blackpool, England. A soldier and statesman, he had been Woodrow Wilson's friend and had endured the failure of the League of Nations with him. In spite of this, there was only one entry beneath his father's name, written by his father: New York to Paris, nonstop, 1927.

Acknowledging the pattern – Charlemagne, the prized horse, the railroad, the airplane –Phil smiled ironically. He moved his coat from the chair and sat down by the window. Taking out his pen, he carefully lettered another entry below his father's, one word, which, in Phil's mind, said it all: Trinity. Only a few moments after this first atomic bomb, he had enlisted in the Army. Where his father's career had ended, his had begun.

Pushing a small indentation on the SMTV strapped to his wrist, he summoned his limousine. He had ten minutes until its arrival. His attaché case lay on the bed, his topcoat and gloves beside it, all that he had been allowed to retain—except the little black book in his hands.

Slowly he turned the page to his own recorded birth. In his father's firm broad stroke was written, Phillip Scott Johnson, IV, b. May 21, 1926, and the stages of his life followed: Volunteered, WWII, May 21, 1944. With Patton, 2nd Lt. Korean War, Capt. 1950. Viet Nam, Lt. Col., 1963. The three wars blurred in his memory, so little time between, so nearly the same, slight change in *geography, slight change in rank, no change in his regimental living. He'd come home at intervals between wars, watched as his father's health deteriorated, recalled his words on that last visit:*

"Son, you need to settle down soon, find yourself an Elizabeth. You're getting on —what, now, forty?"

"Thirty-nine, Dad, and I'm committed for the moment. We're entering a new phase."

"There'll always be a 'new' phase, Son, a new deal, a new frontier. Don't let the important things slide."

He'd been enroute to Cambodia, on special assignment when word came, and he'd completed his mission. He'd been preoccupied, those years, every waking moment dedicated to the Strategic Air Command. SAC had been his wife, his family. Oh, there had been women, several, but his caution had prevented an immediate alliance, and the Cold War had kept him on the move, Europe, the Far East, then South America. Now, alone in his cold hotel room, he heard again his father's words: "Don't let the important things slide, Phil."

He looked down at the small leather-bound volume. The military record was interrupted here, and in Phil's own precise lettering was written: Col. Phillip Scott Johnson, the third, d. Jan 3, 1966. While he was in Nam, agonizing over the decision to bomb or not to bomb. He hadn't gone home. Not then. It was later, when news of his mother's illness reached him, and he'd flown in, met the distant relatives, Texans he'd hardly known, and the little black book had been found in the library desk drawer. His mother, seeing it in his hands, said, "Find a nice girl, Phil. You're getting on."

Phil stood up, put on his coat and adjusted his black silk tie. He pulled the venetian blind to the top of his window and looked out. He understood the connection of the Milstar System, 70,000 miles above the earth, but he had failed to learn the secret of interpersonal relationships. There had been one special lady, a young, slim girl from Boston, and he struggled to recall her name, remembering instead the emotional night he'd –bravely—asked her to' wait for him' while he flew off to the Kwajalein Islands.

"Wait?" she'd said, incredulity in her voice, "Wait! While you traverse the globe, playing your childish war games?"

The word, childish –for something he considered so vital –the word alone cooled his ardor.

Phillip moved away from the high window, away from the massive concrete buildings, away from streets stretching endlessly through the congested city, away from the dark housetops looking like so many Quonset huts lined up in rows. Seven years, and he still missed Alabama, the only home he'd ever owned, comfortable, unpretentious white brick house on a tree-lined street, grass to mow in the summer, leaves to rake in the fall. That had been one important thing he had let slide. The face of his commander came to mind, steel-eyed behind the dark plastic frames. "Don't get too settled, Phil," he'd said, "there's something in the wind, and I know you'll want to be a part of it."

Ruefully, he shook his head. Perhaps he should have kept the house. An image came to mind and he chuckled. Small gold plate on the front door: Once the home of General Phillip Scott Johnson. Open 2 p.m. to 4p.m. His charts, so carefully collected over the years, could have remained on the dark-paneled walls, his books in the walnut shelves, but no, it was best that he dispose of everything himself. Everything except the little black book in his hands. There was a special niche for it in his cocoon—he had designed it so. The warm home in the small southern city he would carry with him, in his mind, a reminder of his days with NASA, a special memory of gentle friends, caring co-workers. Tenderly, he tucked the small book into his attaché case, meticulously rearranging the flat red folders to accommodate its slight addition, closed the top and spun the combination lock into random position. His time was up.

Phil left the hotel room, sensing the thick gray carpet under his feet, feeling its luxurious depth as he walked to the waiting limousine. "Never let the important things slide," his father had said, and once again he was putting first things first.

The twenty-minute drive was made in silence, his driver, young, deferentially addressing him as 'Sir', trained to refrain from idle conversation. As they crossed the Potomac, he noted the water reflecting the gray overcast sky, the bridge one long continuation of gray pavement momentarily suspended: man, once again overcoming natural barriers.

He tapped the young driver on the shoulder, indicated with a gesture that he wanted to disembark at the front entrance to the Pentagon. The walk into Chambers would give him time to review his presentation: underground bunkers, fully supplied and manned, computer terminals linked to spaced satellites, ready to direct nuclear missiles projected from silos and submarines. His "C3I" plan—acronym for command, control, communications and intelligence – America's central nervous system for nuclear war, was now operational. In the event that Washington was destroyed, the President, Vice-President, and Secretary of Defense killed, he already would be aloft, already in command, or if not aloft, deep underground in the Catoctin Mountains.

Phil approached the high brass double doors, transferred his attach` case from his right hand to his left, conscious once again of its weight – a weight he had, ruefully, attributed to its subject until this morning. For the first time it occurred to him that the burden could have something to do with his age. He felt his father's presence and spoke to him apologetically. "Sorry, Father. I guess I let something important slide."

He smiled as he reached the highly polished doors. Somewhere out there, somewhere in those dark-roofed houses were many Elizabeth's, --and Beverly's, Charlottes, and Janes—sleeping sweetly, raising sons and daughters in comparative safety, blissfully unaware of the manned 747's circling ever above them, day and night.

On impulse, he stopped, placed his weighted case on a stainless-steel smoker's stand —empty, now that the government had enforced the ban against smoking — and opened it carefully, extracting the little black book. With a silver Cross pen, he wrote the last entry, on the last page, before tucking it once again into his breast pocket: *February 14, 1994, Looking-Glass Commander-In-Chief, Director of the Black Budget, World War IV.*

He opened the brass doors and faced the assemblage who arose to greet him.

EPILOGUE

LOOK UP

I stood alone upon the hill
The sun upon my face.
I looked into the clouds of light
And tried to find my place.

Someone touched my arm,
spoke softly and said,
"You'll find my kingdom
by looking there instead."

The valley was filled with houses
and people rushed about.
The world lay at my feet,
waiting and spread out.

I looked below where shadows fell
and saw the sun in places,
But the people there
had weary, frowning faces.

Down the hill I had climbed
To join my fellow man.
Stumbled on the rocks and roots
But He took my hand.

I reached the path: He let me go,
yet patient still and kind.

"Look up again, my child." He said,
"whenever you find the time.

~Betty Roberts

"Blue Tree"
Oil on Canvas by Betty Roberts

EXPEDITION: SUCCESSFUL

The old woman pulled her Cardiac Walker closer to the bed. Now, if she was careful, yes, she could reach it. The alarm had been a bit difficult to disarm, but nail clippers had done the trick. Easy, now, slippers first, ah, one on, now the other, yes. Not too difficult now, stand –no bell ringing—it was going to work. One step at a time, refrigerator first, before anyone comes. Quiet, now. Thank goodness for the rubber tires on the walker; this was a state-of-the-art contraption, nothing but the best for you, grandma. The lid raised up, nice little catch-all for all her stolen goodies, like the wine --.

She knew just where it was, the door to the frig had nice, deep shelves, packed with all kinds of things, bottles and jars, once in place seldom used, the wine was in the back, right between the ketchup and the French mustard, black screw-top, looked more like a bottle of hot sauce – oh, Charles, the wines, the wines! Remember?

The small café like in the old song, ah, viva la France. It was so perfect, just the two of us, sneaking away, the narrow streets, the lights along the river, remember, Charles?

The class was dismissed early, another bombing, or a false alarm? She gathered her books, put them in the burlap sack and joined the other students in a slow, but orderly procession to the underground shelter; she was jostled from behind, the book bag flew out of her arms and she hit the concrete stairs head first—the lights went out, she couldn't see, but she could hear, someone helping her up, pulling her into his arms, rough wool coat against her face, holding her tight against his chest—she had no doubt it was a man—the lights came on. She could see. It was a dark-haired boy, one she had noticed days ago, when the class first started.

"I beg your pardon," he said, "are you hurt? My name is Charles."

"No, no, nothing broken, I don't think. My name is Annie.

"Hello, Annie. I intend to be your friend—your best friend," he said, looking deep into her eyes. He smiled, and she was lost. She

knew he had spoken of the future: they would be best friends. It had been a grand five years, the war nearly over, peace now being negotiated, but with bombs still being dropped daily. They had pretended they were tourists—perhaps American tourists—with unlimited money and time on their hands, and every traditional tourist attraction drew them to explore, to laugh, to discover, not only the history, but each other. His fingers running over her, "I love your body, Michelle, your skin is like young peaches, before they are old enough to grow the fuzz, and soft, cloud-white, and the dew in your eyes! Oh, Michelle, Michelle, had I not found you, I would not have lived!"

"My name is Annie," she had said, and he had replied, "But for now, for France, it will be Michelle."

It's true: you never hear the one that kills you. They had not heard the bomb, no streak of sound to follow as it landed on the house next door, Charles thrown, torn away from her arms, the wine—a French rose' I believe it was, hitting the stone floor, spilling, mingling with his blood. He had been her first, the one to pierce the tissue-thin covering and make her know what it was to be a woman, a young woman, a woman in love. There had been many others, but a woman never forgets her first.

The wine was chilled—she'd known it would be, three days, or was it four since she'd first spotted it in the frig? It fit nicely into the small pocket under the seat in her cardiac walker. Now, careful, turn slowly, no point in hurrying, if she was caught, she was caught. Back up the hall, ease into bed, careful, careful, good. Very good. No alarm, pillows piled behind her head. She sipped the wine slowly, holding it in her mouth, savoring the tangy, sparkling flavor, yes, it had been a rose', she was sure, now. She remembered.

Now, to sleep, perhaps to dream . . . expedition: successful.

Now the question becomes, how will I spend my days? Maybe go searching for a third husband? That's a possibility, but instead, maybe I'll turn once again to my computer. There's this box in the closet, letters written or received over the years, either from one husband or the other, or from the lovers in between. Another book? Perhaps a real one, with all the truth that was left out of this one.

Hemingway once said, "...if no nation can exist half free and half slave no man can write half whore and half straight ...." But it might be fun to try. Hum ----.

Now, in Walt Whitman's "brooding and blissful halcyon days, the teeming, quietest, happiest days of all" after a lifetime of postponement, my title has once again changed. Now, I am Ms. Betty Roberts, writer. Or simply, Miss Betty. That's good enough.

MEMORIES

How sweet the silent backward tracing!
The wanderings as in dreams —the
Meditation of old times resumed —
Their loves, joys, persons, voyages.

LEAVES OF GRASS

Walt Whitman (1819-1892)

INDEX OF POEMS

INDEX OF STORIES